A COMPLETE
WASTE OF TIME

A COMPLETE WASTE OF TIME

Tales and Tips about
Getting More Done

Mark Ellwood

Published by Pace Productivity Inc.
TORONTO

First published in 1997 by
Pace Productivity Inc.
47 Kenneth Avenue
Toronto, Canada
M6P 1J1

Canadian Cataloguing in Publication Data

Ellwood, Mark, 1956-
   A complete waste of time : tales and tips about getting more done

ISBN 0-9682395-0-1

1. Time management. I. Title.

HD69.T54E43 1997   650.1   C97-931648-0

Edited by Colborne Communications
Typography and Design by Falcom Design & Communications
Cover Design by Capstone Communications Group
Hugs by Susan
Printed and Bound in Canada by Webcom Limited

97 98 99 00 01 5 4 3 2 1

Contents

PROLOGUE

As a consultant who helps organizations improve their productivity, I'm always looking for ways to teach people how to get more done. There's plenty of information out there, but how could I best communicate it?

It occurred to me that one of the best ways to learn is through stories. If you listen to popular professional speakers and trainers, you'll hear anecdotes sprinkled throughout their presentations. Storytelling is a part of every human culture, going back thousands of years. Stories create an emotional connection. They tap into our subconscious. They reveal what has happened, not just the theory of what might happen. They also create familiarity through characters and situations the reader can connect with.

So let me tell you a tale…

Once Upon a Time...

Once upon a time people enjoyed their jobs. They liked to work hard and they liked to play hard, except when it resulted in shin splints. It was a time of joy and happiness and productivity. People earned lots of money. Some were promoted. The rest went to shopping malls, where they bought tight-fitting shoes and ate from plastic boxes in food courts. People had long, healthy, happy careers with their companies. At night they went home to enjoy their families, their hobbies and their six-cycle washing machines. Everyone liked the way things were.

One day, three sorcerers appeared at the top of a tall tower downtown. They came down from on high to make their prophecies to the people, taking the service elevator, along with the cleaning staff and their carts full of toilet paper rolls. The sorcerers announced that things would get better and better. But the sorcerers turned out to be not as nice as everyone thought, and things got worse.

The first of these nasty sorcerers was named Technomighty. He decreed that all people had to attach themselves to little communication machines. People were supposed to place one end of the device next to their ear and talk into the other end. At first the people thought doing this was really special. They would talk in their TellyFonies walking down the street, while sitting in movie theaters and while eating in restaurants where waiters put napkins in people's laps for them. They would also talk to their TellyFonies in the middle of meetings, on vacation or even in bed while they were making Yunowatt.

The nasty sorcerer Technomighty also made people attach their fingers to plastic machines with little buttons on which letters were printed. While tapping on these buttons, people had to stare at screens covered with words. Some people didn't like doing this, so they played Solitaire instead. And all those waiters had trouble giving people their napkins because their lap tops were covered with laptops.

The second nasty sorcerer was named Globissa Maxima. She said, "You must run all over the world. You must take things from here and give them to people in distant lands. You will get lots of money in return." She told the people they had to think about being global. Some of them thought she said gullible. Then she issued another decree: "The world is your oyster, so I hope you like seafood." Everyone was supposed to talk to people in distant lands with their TellyFonies. But sometimes they forgot that time zones were different there, and they woke up people who were busy making Yunowatt.

Everyone was supposed to go on long voyages to distant lands. They traveled far and wide on large, noisy machines with wings, where the big thrill was putting hot napkins on their faces and eating tiny pieces of cheese wrapped in plastic. This was supposed to be another special thing. And the people had to embrace big words such as globalizationism and competitiveness. Globissa Maxima encouraged people to merge and acquire and then to tell their employees that it would be business as usual, even though it never was.

The third nasty sorcerer was named Consultalot. Consultalot

was an it, rather than a he or a she. It scattered all kinds of letters over the land, such as TQM and BPR and ROI. Then it made people send useless stuff to one another FYI. It made up new words like down-size and right-size and shoe-size. It also liked to put words together without any adjectives. People used to say things like "pretty blue sky." Now they could talk only in long strings of nouns like "Systems Integration Management Procedures." And Consultalot got paid for making fancy presentations on big screens with lots of Venn diagrams and flow charts and too many colors.

Because of the three nasty sorcerers, people were working harder and harder and not watching situation comedies as much anymore. They also had trouble managing their time. Most ran out of time, so they had to take out loans and live on borrowed time. And everyone was supposed to embrace change. But no one had enough money even to make change. Many people were overworked, underpaid, overstressed and underground. As a gift for all their extra work, Consultalot let some of them wear sports shirts and running shoes on Fridays. This reward, too, was supposed to be special. But nobody really felt special at all.

Then hope arose in the kingdom. Now and then a brave knight with a funny name such as Crispin Quirty came along and said, "Wait a minute," even though that was a long time to wait when everyone was rushing around so much. He said, "Maybe we can take control of our own lives. Maybe we can improve how we spend our time. Maybe I'll be a little less vague in my next sentence."

He spread the good word. The word was "undergarment." He reminded people that their jobs could be enriching once again and that they could improve themselves, despite the nasty sorcerers. Once again, people could manage their time and enjoy their work. They could get more balance in their life so they would have more time to play with their little ones, to help their community groups and to add to their swizzle stick collections. He discovered that the little changes people make in their lives are just as important as the big changes that other people impose on them. He believed that the workplace should be pleasant and productive. He reminded everyone that they were special after all. So they all lived happily ever after, at least until Tuesday.

In the introduction to The Art of Fiction, R.F. Dietrich and Roger H. Sundell talk about the importance of creating myth and fiction in our lives:

> In its broadest sense, a fiction is any imaginative re-creation or reconstruction of life…The writer of fiction owes no allegiance except to the reality he seeks to represent, and if he must rearrange the mere surface facts of chaotic human existence into meaningful order for the sake of exposing the facts of life occurring beneath the surface, the reader should not condemn the storyteller for abandoning "reality," but rather he should thank the teller for making him see and know the more significant reality that is invisible to the ordinary eye.

That is what these tales attempt to do. This book is all about the stories of work — the stories of your friends, colleagues, bosses, co-workers and subordinates. And, I hope, there's a touch of humor to these stories as well. Each story is based on the kinds of issues you might face in getting things done at work or at home. If you've ever wondered how to make better use of your time, you'll enjoy reading these lighthearted anecdotes about work life.

Each story deals with a different aspect of productivity,

including holding effective meetings, dealing with walk-in visitors, and avoiding procrastination. The stories do not use traditional case studies. Rather, they use humor, character and plot to convey their message. The stories all feature someone you might know. Time management has never before been so much fun, and each story takes just a few minutes to read.

Each tale finishes with a short moral in the form of a rhyming couplet. Each is followed by a How To article filled with tips that connect with the story. The tips provide steps that you can follow immediately to use your time more effectively.

Over the last eight years, I've been consulting and training in productivity enhancement. From presidents to managers to sales reps to service clerks, everyone seems to be pressed for time. And everyone would like to create just a little more balance in their lives. In consulting with clients, our company has gathered research data about the use of time, based on an electric device I developed in 1989 called the TimeCorder®. The TimeCorder® is a user-friendly device similar to a stopwatch which allows employees to track their time. Most people find using the TimeCorder® enjoyable and insightful. Some of the research from our database, as well as information from other sources, is included in the Time Trivia sections to provide further enlightenment.

As you read the stories, you may see yourself in them, or you may see someone else with whom you can identify. That's the easy part. The hard part is committing to improve. Choose one or two themes per week, and commit to making just a couple of improvements at a time. And remember that changing habits doesn't happen overnight. If you can do something differently for about a month, you'll create a new habit. Then you'll be set for life.

Read, discover and learn. Then take control of your time. But don't wait. Start today. Your time is worth it.

PLANNING AHEAD

In reality, killing time is only the name for another of the multifarious ways by which Time kills us. SIR OSBERT SITWELL

Fairy Godmothers
Don't Have Mortgages

According to Adrian Pritlove's horoscope, this would be his lucky week. Early Monday morning, he sat at his desk and began writing his weekly goals in bold letters on a blank sheet of paper: GOAL: Win a million dollars.

He smiled to himself, just as Serena Glowing, one of his co-workers, approached his desk. She had long, curly, blonde hair and an inner glow that made her look like a fairy godmother in a radiant, attractive sort of way. Radiantly, she glanced at Adrian's sheet.

"That's not a goal," said Serena.

"No, it's a piece of paper."

"Yes, of course. But what's that you've written on it?" she asked.

"Words. English. A well-known language circa late twentieth century, known for..."

"Yes, I can see that. But that's not a goal, the million dollars part. If you can't make it happen, then it's a wish, not a goal. Unless you have some sort of personal relationship with a fairy godmother." Adrian turned a shade of red and flipped the sheet over in embarrassment. His horoscope hadn't counted on this.

"OK. Well, how do I make a wish?"

"It's not that easy. Not while the astral plane is out of alignment with the earth's recessional aura, anyway."

"I've got Saturday off. Can it happen then?" Adrian asked, perplexed.

"Actually, it's not for a while." She quickly changed the subject. "So why do you want to win a million dollars? You've got a fine job here at the Peabody Proud Pencil Division."

"Yes," said Adrian, regretting the effect of the alliterative name as he wiped away the tiny droplets that Serena had unwittingly projected onto his sheet. "But I do have a rather hefty mortgage on my house. I don't like the idea of being burdened with all that debt. Even a small prize, say ten thousand, would help pay it off."

"Ten thousand? That's nothing. You can save ten, twenty, thirty thousand, without having to shell out for all those long-shot lottery tickets you keep buying."

"Oh, but I have a scientific system!" Adrian's system consisted of a computerized regression analysis of previous winners, a pair of dice and a rabbit foot key chain.

"Your system and a quarter will get you…well, something that costs a quarter, I guess. Now, let's just get this straight. What is your goal?"

"Fast cars. Yachts. A dog named 'Get Lost.' Then I can say, 'Come here, Get Lost.'"

"Yes but realistically…"

"Well, I suppose it would be nice to pay off my mortgage."

"Why's that?"

"So I can have more money for my hobby. I make scale models of sewage treatment plants."

"Wanting more disposable income is a short-term goal. Paying off your mortgage is a long-term goal. And there are different ways of doing that. Like paying weekly instead of monthly. The more frequently the interest is compounded, the faster your mortgage goes down. That will save you thousands over the years of your mortgage." Serena was beginning to sound like a banker, which normally requires a considerable knowledge of how to be dull, particularly on days of the week that end in the letter y. Adrian's eyes began to glaze over as she continued. "Or you could increase your payments by just a bit when your mortgage is renewed."

"Wait a minute. I wanted more money, not less," said Adrian.

"Yes, but do you want more money today or more money over the long term?"

"Today!"

"Then you need a different strategy. You see, your goal is what you want; your strategy is how you get there. So maybe a part-time job would help you achieve your short-term goal of having more money."

"Yeah, I heard they're hiring down at the Yum Yum Tastee Treet. I always thought there was a future for me in ice cream treats."

Serena left Adrian to ponder his plans. A week later he began a part-time job delivering flyers for a local fitness club. (Burn Fat Now, and Your Friends Will Be Burning with Envy!!) His cash flow improved. Serena had hit the nail on the head with her advice. She was pretty good with a drill press, too.

A week later Adrian crumpled up his old goal sheet and tossed it at the garbage can, missing it, as usual. Then he noticed a gold-colored baton in the corner of his cubicle. He began a new goal sheet, writing in large broad strokes, Find additional part-time income opportunities. Then, in smaller letters, Take Serena out to lunch. Return her wand.

Determine your goals, they're what you desire,
Develop a plan and get out of the mire.

SET GOALS

The pursuit of excellence is gratifying and healthy; the pursuit of perfection is frustrating, neurotic, and a terrible waste of time. ANONYMOUS

To use your time effectively tomorrow, you need to determine your goals today. The goals you set are your pictures of success. Without goals, also known as objectives, you can't know whether your activities are effective or, as time management expert Alec Mackenzie says, "whether a given decision is right or useless. When the objective hasn't been set, you can't know when you've achieved it, and you can't measure progress along the way... When we don't have priorities of our own, we say yes to too many requests of others...When we don't impose deadlines on ourselves, we may never get around to the real priority for the day—because we never have time to get everything done."

That's why you should establish your goals for the long term, say one to five years, and for the short term over the next few months. You also need to write these goals down. Successful people always identify their goals, whether they are daily, yearly or lifelong goals.

But a goal shouldn't just be "I want to lose weight" or "I hope to be rich someday." Those goals are too vague, and are more like New Year's resolutions—well intentioned but short on substance. Resolutions aren't specific. They are usually associated with no commitment and no plans for follow-through.

So use a handy acronym known as SMART to determine your goals. This acronym stands for Specific, Measurable, Appropriate, Realistic and Time-bound.

Specific Goals

Goals such as being happy, getting rich or simply having a good time lack specificity. But goals such as getting married, earning more money and taking regular vacations have more definition.

The s in 'Specificity' also stands for 'Substantial.' This kind of goal is concrete and worthy of pursuit. You might decide that keeping the kitchen clean is a goal. But it's not the sort of life accomplishment you would want to be praised for in your epitaph. If cleanliness is an issue, then certainly establish a goal to improve. But put it in context with more important pursuits. What will you be proud of five years from now? What kinds of things would you like to boast about in your annual Christmas cards or newsletters? If you had to write a resumé about your life, what would you want to put in it? Your accomplishments would be based on goals that are specific and substantial.

Measurable Goals

The second criteria a goal should meet is measurability. You should state your goal in such a way that an outside observer could measure it objectively. For instance, the following goals are measurable:

"I will take two vacations this year."

"I will earn $100,000 by March."

"I will stop smoking in two months."

You can see what happens when you combine the criterion of specificity with measurability. For instance, you might decide that your target is to learn a new language by September. This goal certainly meets the criterion of being measurable. However, it isn't very specific, because it doesn't say what language you will learn or to what degree you will learn it. So, put the two criteria together. "My goal is to learn French sufficiently to be able to take a vacation in France in October without having to speak any English."

The same goal might be measured in a number of ways. For instance, a sales rep might aim for specific sales dollars generated, profit for the territory, introductions of new products and increase in distribution channels. It's possible that she would be successful in one criterion, but not in another. Another example involves a fund-raising charity auction. It drew hundreds of people (above target), and obtained broad media exposure (above target), but it raised only a few dollars (below target). That doesn't mean the event was unsuccessful—it just didn't meet all of its goals. Understanding the results for a project on different goals that were established will give the organizers valuable input and guidance if they are to repeat the event the following year of different goals that were established.

Appropriate Goals

An appropriate goal is within your grasp. It should be within your area of power or responsibility. Don't try to work on someone else's goals. Achievable goals are consistent with your organization's aims, culture or standards. For instance, don't aim to increase customer satisfaction (a goal) with longer credit terms (a strategy) when the company is trying to reduce its accounts receivable (another goal).

Appropriate goals also relate to your personal style. What are you capable of accomplishing, given your background, your skills, your training or even your physical makeup? People who are only five feet tall have little chance of making the Olympic basketball team.

That's not to say you shouldn't extend yourself. It is possible to go beyond anything you've done before, and to push yourself past the limits you thought were unsurpassable. It is possible to stretch your imagination to conquer heights you thought were unreachable. Allow your dreams to flourish. But make sure you have the resources, time and makeup to turn your dreams into reality.

Realistic Goals

Make sure that your goals can be met. A goal might be achievable within the next three months, but this deadline may be unrealistic, given the other constraints you're facing. In your business, don't aim for a market share that is simply not going to happen. Don't plan to learn Chinese if you have no intention of going to China or of dealing with Chinese people. Don't expect to renovate your basement in a weekend.

How do you know what is realistic? Look for relevant comparisons. Examine historical trends. What has been done in the past? Or look at economic indicators. What are the trends for the future? What has the competition been able to achieve? Has someone else embarked on a similar journey whose results might indicate what is possible?

A dose of good old gut feeling also helps. Tripling your salary in your current job by the end of this year is a specific and measurable goal. But it's not very realistic if you are earning minimum wage by washing dishes at the local greasy spoon. In that case, perhaps your goal should be to find a higher-paying job or to start your own business.

Time-bound Goals

Put a deadline on your goals—this Saturday, the end of the month, the end of the year, your fiftieth birthday, whatever. Start with the end in mind. What will the final picture of success look like and when do you want it to happen? By determining the end time, you can then work your way backwards to see what you need to do by then.

The challenge you'll face is that the goal may seem huge and you just don't know where to begin. That's when you break larger goals into smaller ones, creating milestones to achieve along the way.

There is one character who does this better than anyone else, and who is probably the greatest time manager of all time. He is the jolly old man who brings joy to so many lives: Santa Claus. This fellow has a huge task to do, all in one night. He knows his target date, and there can be no delays, extensions or missed appointments. So from Christmas Eve, he needs to work backwards and create a list of minor goals and targets that all lead up to the big event.

SANTA'S GOALS

Determine gift forecast	*February*
Purchase raw materials	*March*
Create production timetable	*April*
Have elves produce presents	*May*
Complete contracts for photo shoots	*June*
Order gift wrap	*September*
Begin present wrapping	*October*
Attend media appearances, parades	*November*
Match presents to lists received	*December 1*
Wrap presents	*December 15*
Conduct final reindeer training run	*December 22*
Load sleigh	*December 23*
Sally forth!	*December 24*

(You'll notice there are no goals for January. That's because Santa needs a vacation too.)

Passion

The SMART acronym is missing one last letter, p for 'Passion.'

Pursue your goals with passion! Don't become complacent about not meeting them. For example, saying "We didn't meet our goal last month, but that's all right, we'll make up for it" should never be good enough. Rework your goals if necessary, but pursue them with a renewed vigor and with a sincere desire to succeed.

TIME TRIVIA

The typical manager spends 3½ hours per week on planning-related activities. That represents 7% of an average 52-hour work week. Managing people and projects takes another 8¾ hours, or 17% of the work week.
PACE PRODUCTIVITY RESEARCH

Chief Cook and
Bottle Washer

G erald McGuckin recently had an interesting fantasy. It was bizarre and extreme—something completely out of the ordinary for him. He would make dinner for one of his dates.

Usually, whenever he said "Let's go to my house for dinner," he was really saying, "Let me show you what an idiot I am." After all, the only things Gerald made well were reservations. His culinary experience was limited to assembling salads at the local burger joint's salad bar.

He had tried to teach himself to cook once. He was the only person who had ever gone to a self-help book for advice and been turned down.

Nevertheless, it was time to turn his fantasy into a reality. First he had to invite someone. He decided to ask Jasmine Foxwell over for dinner, and she accepted. When she arrived at Gerald's apartment, her first order of business was to check the place out. This was a woman who had a thing about men's leaving toilet seats up all the time. So she had brought along her own fluffy toilet seat cover. Her inspection tour continued in the kitchen, where she took inventory. Gerald's kitchen was entirely stocked with gadgets advertised on late-night television. Apparently, he would write the manufacturers a letter, saying,

"Never mind all the carving knives and kitchen wizards, can you just send me all the stuff that comes free with them?" As a result, he ended up with nineteen potato peelers.

Gerald had also attempted to make his kitchen more high tech. Once when the timer on his oven had broken, he had connected the oven to his VCR control. As a timer, this system was quite ingenious. However, putting the VCR in the oven rather than on it might not have been the wisest move. Of course, that was nothing compared to what had happened when he connected the doorbell to the toilet.

It was time to prepare dinner, and Gerald decided to try an omelet. Unfortunately, getting the eggs out of their shell was not something he was terribly good at. He was generally terribly bad at it.

Jasmine suggested tapping the eggs gently against a sharp edge, such as the lip of the pan. Gerald did as instructed. Half the shell fell into the saucepan and the other half, plus egg, fell somewhere in the nether world of the electric burner. The next time he tried it, he got half the egg plus half the shell into the saucepan.

Jasmine, slightly exasperated, instructed him to crack the shell lightly, then gently pry his thumbs into the crack and pull steadily apart. This technique worked wonderfully. Too bad he hadn't done it over the pan, though.

Gerald finally discovered his own technique. He simply stood over the pan with the egg held firmly in his hand and squeezed. The runny stuff seeped between his fingers onto the pan and the shell was retained. Or some of it was.

Eventually, dinner was cooked and served, except for the black bits. At the dinner table, Gerald attempted some idle chit chat. He had difficulty getting Jasmine's attention though, as she was immersed in reading a warehouse shelving catalog. So Gerald struck up a conversation with the alphabet soup.

After they finished eating, Gerald asked, "Did you like the food?"

"As French toast goes, it wasn't bad," she responded.

"You know, I kind of enjoy this cooking thing," Gerald said. "I could probably make a good chef someday. I just might take it up. I love the vagueness, the artistry of it all. A pinch of salt, a dash of pepper, a smidgen of garlic, a gentle stirring, a generous sprinkling. It's all so…so…what's that French word, hors d'oeuvre? I'd love to run a restaurant, be the talk of the town. By the way, how much is a smidgen anyway?"

"Just a little less than what you know. I suppose if you wanted to be a cook you could become one. But you might want to perfect your boiled eggs first," said Jasmine.

It has been said that sex and culinary delights are often linked. So after Jasmine left, Gerald decided that his next sexual fantasy and his next cooking fantasy would be linked together, and he signed up for a course called "Intimate evenings for one."

When deciding your future, do what you know best
Your knowledge and skills will be put to the test.

MAKE A MAJOR LIFE
OR CAREER DECISION

---

*One never rises so high as when one does not
know where one is going.* OLIVER CROMWELL

So you're thinking about making a big change. New job, new
city, new career, new education. First ask yourself, "Am I happy
with where I am now?" If not, what are the key factors I need to
change? Salary, responsibility, boss, industry, self-image, fitness?
Perhaps you're dissatisfied. But what will guide you in deciding
how to change? Your choice should be based on your own life
mission. Companies have missions and so can individuals. Your
mission reflects your purpose—the ideology that guides you in
making day-to-day decisions, as well as long-term plans.
Examples of personal mission statements are:

- I want to create great wealth by providing a needed product
  or service.
- I want to improve the environment, thereby making the
  world a better place to live.
- I care most about other people and endeavor to help them
  improve their lives.
- My family comes before everything else and is the center of
  my life.
- I want to explore the world and learn as much as I can about it.

If you don't have a sense of purpose, make it your goal to find one, perhaps in the next 12 months. Read the paper, go shopping, talk to friends, go on a vacation, read books on changing careers and go to networking events to find what interests you. Find something you love, and devote yourself to it.

Keep involved with a satisfying short-term project while determining your new long-term direction, so that you're engaged with meaningful activity. For instance, appear in a community play, train for a marathon or volunteer for a charity fundraiser while job searching or educating yourself.

When you're close to deciding on a big change, ask yourself how consistent it is with your life mission. Determine whether your new direction is in keeping with your:

- *Skills.* Are you a good leader, accountant, sales person, organizer or manager?
- *Habits or behaviors.* Do you like working evenings or traveling? Do you work best on your own or in a group? Are you social? Do you need to sleep in? Do you have family commitments that affect your decisions?
- *Values.* Do you care about products that help the environment? Is money less important than influence or prestige? Do you operate from a position of high integrity?
- *Goals.* Where do you want to be? Do you want to double your salary in the next two years? How much vacation time would you like?

Consider whether the decision about your new direction also avoids your weaknesses and dislikes. For instance, do you abhor office politics? Do you tend to do things your own way? Do you need lots of direction? Are you in the right physical condition for this new direction?

What are the short-term versus long-term issues? Maybe a new job doesn't pay the salary you want. But it may open up a new career direction or lead to promotion in the near future.

Careers are no longer for life, so you can always change later. Never turn down a job because the money falls short by 10 or 15 percent if it's something you truly love and if it may open up later possibilities.

Most of all, ask yourself what your gut feeling is. If you have to think about it too much or rationalize a mediocre decision, then the change is probably not for you.

TIME TRIVIA

The 40 hour work week is definitely not a reality for most workers. Following are how long people spend on work related activities each week, including the time they spend after hours or on weekends:

Position	Hours per week
Independent consultants	63
Sales managers	50
Truck drivers on local delivery	49
Outside sales reps	47
Inside sales reps	46
Warehouse workers	45
Bankers (including clerical staff)	44
Administrative support staff	44

PACE PRODUCTIVITY RESEARCH

Something Sounds Fishy— It Could Be the Fish

Mermaids and sea serpents were taking up far too much of Sherwood Doddridge's time. Lorilee was one of his favorite mermaids, with her long, flowing, auburn hair, her friendly brown eyes and her variegated golden scales. She also a spike protruding from her plastic tail, which was ideal for placing her in the sand at the bottom of the aquarium, right next to the acrylic sea serpent.

Sherwood, a forty-two-year-old accounting manager, was the company's self-proclaimed zoo keeper. Taking care of the tank in the lobby was his favorite chore, along with sorting his supply of paper clips. Lorilee was Sherwood's latest decorative acquisition: Mermaid, Model 3CBF5—auburn. On this day, his routine was the same as always. First he read the morning paper, briefly browsing through the births, pensively perusing the personals and casually consuming the comics.

After reading the paper, Sherwood amused himself by hunting for typographical errors in the company's policy manuals. The next urgent matter involved reorganizing his desk. Sherwood took all the small piles of files, magazines, forms, slips, reports and fish food catalogs and stacked them into one large pile. This created a relatively clean surface on his desk.

Then he restacked everything into smaller piles of things to read, things to put off and things he wasn't sure about. The last pile was usually the largest. On rare occasions, the odd item ended up in the garbage bin. The even items didn't even make the cut. The net effect of this ritual was to completely cover Sherwood's desk again. Flat surfaces were tantalizing to him as hungry voids of empty space desirous to be filled—sort of like suburbia, only more exciting.

Out of the blue, his assistant suddenly dropped in. The couch cushioned her fall. She deposited a stack of magazines, correspondence, out-of-date reports and this month's copy of *Plant World* in Sherwood's already overstuffed in basket.

She was about to leave when she said, "Hey, I heard a great joke on the Late Late Late Show last night."

"Uh, huh," said Sherwood.

"Oh, do you want to hear it?"

"Do I have any other options?"

"OK, well you see these three guys walk into a bar. And one of them says… No wait, I have to tell you who they are. There's a lawyer, a farmer and a priest. Anyway, the priest… No wait. I think it was the lawyer. Anyway he says to the bartender… Or wait, is that right? Actually the bartender says to him. 'Do you want a number fifty five?' Oh, just a sec. No it was the… Wait."

"A lot of waiting in this joke, it seems," said Sherwood sardonically.

"Well there's a great punch line. The bartender says, 'When you get there, make mine a twenty-seven.'" She began to laugh hysterically. "It was really funny."

"Oh, yeah, I'm in stitches," said Sherwood.

She left, giggling and repeating the punch line to herself. Sherwood hardly saw her leave though. The pile in his In Basket was high enough to block the view of his doorway. He began to eagerly sort through the stack of stuff, adding to his existing piles, while creating a new one on the floor near the door.

If only he could get time to sort through it all, he might be able to prepare the performance reviews that were due three days ago.

Just then Sherwood spotted Crispin Quirty, the company's improvement guru, walking by. "Crispin, could I get your help for a minute?" he pleaded.

Crispin Quirty was tall and in his early forties. He had a fashion sense that seemed to have been inspired by Dr. Seuss. He wore a bright red bow tie, which occasionally began to blink. His yellow polka-dot shirt clashed vehemently with slightly short, striped green pants. Evidently, he had confused the dress code with Morse code. Fashion notwithstanding, or not with sitting for that matter, he was well respected for his organizational insights.

Quirty entered Sherwood's office and tripped across a pile of magazines, scattering them on the floor.

"Sorry I knocked those over," he said, as he attempted to restack various back issues of *Goldfish Monthly*. "You seem to have a lot of work here."

"Well, I'm making progress," said Sherwood, "though I'm not sure if I'm getting anywhere."

"Don't worry," Crispin countered sarcastically, "If you don't know where you're going, any path will take you there."

"But I've been so busy. All these reports to read. Requests for licorice-flavored pencil erasers to approve. People keep sending me E-mails about budgets or something. And the aquarium. By the time I get to work on anything, it's coffee break. I hardly even have time for that any more."

"Well, do you have a plan? What's your major goal for today?" Crispin asked, as he tossed aside a tattered copy of *Aquarium Mermaids*.

"I don't have time for making goals."

"So make time. The key is to choose a few vital tasks you have to do and set aside time for them. Ask yourself, 'What is the most important use of my time right now?' It's not sorting through all those papers, and it's certainly not attending another meeting for the Potted Plants Proliferation Program committee."

"But what about the fish? They have to be fed."

"Someone else should be doing that. And stop spending all that time with those aquarium catalogs and mermaid books. And do you really have to count out all those food pellets?"

"No, but I have to…"

"No ifs, ands or buts. That's one word I don't like to hear."

"That was three words."

"There you go, counting again. Cut it out. So what are you going to do now?"

"Make a plan. And make it work. Thanks. See you at coffee break… no wait, I'll skip coffee today."

Sherwood's planning immediately improved. The junk piles disappeared. The fish lived. And Lorilee the mermaid began dating Captain Nemo from the underwater submarine. But that's another story.

Planning's a habit you do every day,
Write it all down, then get on your way.

CREATE STRATEGIES AND PLANS

The first step in effective planning is goal setting, which is covered in the previous section. Your goal represents what you want to do—the result you're seeking, or your destination. But how will you get there? That's where your strategy comes in. Determining a strategy is the second step in planning.

A strategy indicates the course you are going to take. For instance, a retail store has a goal of increasing its sales by 20 percent. One way to achieve this goal is to get current customers to come back more often. Attracting new customers would be a different strategy, though it is possible for the two to work hand in hand. Each strategy will result in different plans: flyers and newsletters will bring back current customers, and advertising will attract first-time shoppers.

Determine the Right Strategy

When determining the right strategy, always ask yourself the question, "How do I want to get there?" Strategies are like policies. They are self-imposed restrictions that channel action along certain lines. They indicate how you will efficiently allocate your limited resources. After all, you can't do everything, so you need to make some choices about how you will reach your goals. Here are some strategic decisions you will need to make in running a business:

- Advertising strategy: What message do you want to leave with your target audience? What media will you use to reach them?
- Distribution strategy. How will people be able to buy your products? Through stores, mail order, the Internet, multi-level marketing, consumer shows, trade shows or infomercials?
- Personnel strategy. What kinds of employees do you want to attract in terms of education, experience or values?
- Research and development. What commitment will you make to new product development?
- Service strategy. What decision-making authority will you give employees to meet customer needs?
- Manufacturing. What will your company make itself and what will it purchase from an outside supplier?
- Information technology. What needs to be automated or computerized? How will automation create a strategic advantage?

Strategies at Home

Establishing strategies for your life outside of work is important, too. Once your strategy is clear, making both day-to-day and long-term decisions becomes much easier.

- Vacations. What kind of vacation do you like? Energetic or relaxing? Popular or out of the way? Will you travel to different spots each year or invest in a summer cottage?
- Television. How do you want your children watching television? For entertainment, education, current events? What time limits should you impose?
- Money. What kinds of investments should you make? Conservative, risky? What type of portfolio is appropriate?
- Location. What kind of area do you want to live in? Does commuting to work play a part?
- Community. Do you donate time or money to local charities? Which type do you support?

Once you've established your goals and strategies, it's time to make a plan. This starts with a project list.

Make Project Lists

For each of your major goals, you should have a project list that outlines a series of steps to get you there. This should be written down. It is not a daily to-do list. That comes later. A project list includes long-term areas of concentration. Some people call it a master list.

Write or type the projects you want to complete over the next one to six months on a sheet of paper. For instance, let's say you want to build an extension to your home, adding an extra family room by the end of the year. This is your goal. You then determine your strategy. Will you build it yourself or hire a contractor? Having decided to build it yourself, you then create a project list, or a master list. Here's what it might look like:

- Write out list of needs and wants for the extension.
- Investigate sub-contractors.
- Determine budget.
- Find an architect.
- Develop plans/drawings/specifications.
- Buy materials and tools.
- Arrange for permits.
- Prepare foundation.
- Erect framing.
- Rough in electrical and plumbing.
- Build roof.
- Install windows and doors.
- Finish interior insulation and drywalls.
- Paint.
- Decorate and furnish.

Each step might have a series of smaller steps attached. Also, you should attach a rough timetable to the list. This is your project list, and you can cross off items as you complete them.

Eventually, the activities on your project list will be transferred onto your daily to-do list. Keep your project list separate from your to-do list. Delete items when they're completed and add new ones when they come up.

TIME TRIVIA

After two decades of exploding growth in computers, economists are confounded by the absence of any apparent payoff in productivity growth. From 1961–1973, the productivity of labor and capital in 18 industrialized countries increased by an average of 2.4% a year. From 1974 to 1992, the international average was only 0.9%.

THE GLOBE AND MAIL, REPORT ON BUSINESS

Ode to a Time Planner

Come hither my friend, I'll show you my book,
You need not be shy, just come have a look.

It's covered with leather and inside you'll see,
The schedules and sheets that should set me free.

I got it last month and started off well,
To use it each day, I thought would be swell.

Up here in the front there's a pocket for stuff,
You can put lots of things, there's room for enough.

For credit cards, cash or an auto receipt,
Coupons, and cash, it's really quite neat.

Divided by sections, it's quite a thick tome,
I take it to work, then carry it home.

I've written my goals and a personal plan,
To lose lots of weight and to get a great tan.

My objective this year was to start to improve,
To really learn more and to get on the move.

I'm not too religious, I'm not into prayer,
But my book is my bible, so I treat it with care.

Though lately I've found, I've skipped now and then,
The time to make plans, I'll start once again.

I must plan for each month, each week and each day,
There isn't much time, but I must find a way.

Though I wonder sometimes if it seems a bit much,
To be writing and copying and listing and such.

The occasional time it becomes like a chore,
This tracking of tasks can be quite a bore.

Perhaps all the time I spend on this thing,
Would be better off spent on learning to sing.

Or to go for a sail, or to drive in my car,
Or watch some TV, or hang out in a bar.

My laziness begs me to throw it away,
This planning is tough on a do-nothing day.

Why write things down when they're all in my head,
I can always remember the things that were said.

Except now and then when I'm late for a date,
I suppose it won't matter, they'll just have to wait.

I'm so busy these days, I don't get the time,
Can't plan my day well, it seems such a crime.

I've let myself down, I've committed a sin,
They say I don't know the trouble I'm in.

Well maybe I'll use it some more in a week,
Or perhaps in a month, my planner I'll seek.

Someday in a while I'll use it much more,
When I figure out what all the pages are for.

CHOOSE A TIME PLANNER

In New York, people are very overbooked.
You say, "When do you want to have dinner?"
It's May. They say, "What about October?"
And then they complain: "Oh you can't
believe how booked up I am." FRAN LEBOWITZ

Time planners come in different shapes and sizes. It doesn't matter what type you choose. The key is to use your planner, not let it sit in a desk drawer.

When you're considering a time-planning system, first consider whether you want compactness or versatility. What you gain in portability, you might give up in the level of detail. Whichever system you choose, make sure it includes a place for your goals, an appointment calendar, a list of contacts, a to-do list and a way of recording progress on your project list.

The secret isn't really the type of planner you choose. It's the discipline you bring to using it. At the very least, be sure to put your goals in writing, whether they relate to your lifelong mission or to your daily to-do list. Use the parts that you really need, and don't worry if you don't use all the sections.

A list follows of the popular types of planners, along with the pros and cons of each.

Pocket Planners

These are roughly four-by-six-inch booklets that can fit in a jacket pocket or a purse. The small size is handy, but it also means that the writing space is limited, which is a problem if you have more than three appointments in a day that you need to cram in. The limited space is even more of a problem when you need to write complex instructions on how to get somewhere.

Desk Planners

Some people still use $8\frac{1}{2}$-by-11-inch books, which sit on the desk and can be carried in a briefcase. Desk planners have more space to write details of appointments, directions and other details. However, they generally lack many of the features that other systems have, such as an address list and room for project lists and long-term goals.

Time Management Binders

These leather-bound books typically contain $5\frac{1}{2}$-by-$8\frac{1}{2}$ inch pages and can be up to a few inches thick. They look very professional and show others that you're a dedicated user. They're convenient, with sections for goals, to-do lists, daily, weekly and monthly scheduling and phone numbers. The book is part of a system; most companies that sell them position themselves as training organizations or change agents. Their seminars, up to a day long, promote basic time management principles. The leather binder is simply a tool to help people better organize themselves.

The books are the ghetto blasters of time management. If you were to buy a home entertainment system, you'd probably buy separate components: a CD player, receiver, speakers and possibly an equalizer. But for portability, you'd buy a ghetto blaster. What you gain in portability, you give up in quality.

The same goes for time management binders. This isn't to say that leather-bound time planners aren't quality products. They are. However, it's difficult to include an entire business plan in one, particularly if you've printed out your plan on full-size paper. Also, the contact management section is limited to names listed in alphabetical order. Although no worse than other systems, a hand-written list of contacts is less flexible than computerized contact management software.

Another drawback is that there is often a lot of recopying involved. You first create monthly goals, which are then transferred onto your weekly list, then transferred again onto your daily list. Planning ahead is also awkward, as you have to switch from one section to another. Thus, many people don't use some of the sections.

One last shortfall to the leather binders is that they are too bulky to throw into a briefcase.

Palm Top Computers

Electronic devices, which are about the same size as pocket planners, are also easy to fit in a jacket pocket or a purse. They run on batteries and have an alpha-numeric keyboard and a small LCD display screen. Some have a screen that you can write on with a special pen. The software translates your printed letters into typewritten characters. Most can store telephone numbers, addresses and notes, and in some cases, they can be downloaded to your main computer, so that you can get a printout. Some also include cards for translation, accounting and other functions.

The challenge with these systems is that scheduling is tricky because of the unit's miniature size. It's hard to type quickly, since the keyboard is small. The screen is also small, so you can't get a quick picture of your schedule for the whole week. When appointments are shown, it's difficult to tell at a glance how long they are if you're using a calendar function. Finally, database functions for contact management are limited. You may not get the same depth of information as you would on a full-size database.

PC-Based Planners

Calendar and scheduling software is also available for your computer. Some scheduling programs stand alone. Others are connected to contact-management systems. You create a database of your contacts, then each time you speak with one, you schedule a subsequent follow-up letter or appointment. These dates become the basis for your planning calendar.

The advantage of computer programs is that they allow you to network with others. That means other people can see your schedule and, in some cases, can book meetings for you. (Maybe that's a disadvantage!) Another benefit is that you can make printouts of your appointments and place them into your planning book. So you've got the automation of a computer combined with the tactility of paper. The drawback is that even if you're using a laptop you have to boot up your laptop to access your calendar, which takes a lot longer than looking in a handy book.

Finally, from a value-added standpoint, your computer doesn't really add much when it is used for scheduling. It simply acts as a typewriter to make your entries look neat.

So there's no one planning tool that is perfect. After all, planning systems aren't distinguished by their features as much as by the people who use them. Choose one, practice using it regularly and you'll find your productivity will increase.

TIME TRIVIA

Among those who watch television, men watch for 23.1 hours per week and women watch for 20.3 hours per week.

STATISTICS CANADA, GENERAL SOCIAL SURVEY

Up the Creek
without a Poodle

There was something odd about my day at work today. I can't quite put my finger on it, but in a strange way I felt as though I were tangled in a web, caught in a trap of overwhelming cliches from which there was no escape. Let me explain.

It all started when I arrived right on the nose at 9:00 a.m. and began some heavy number crunching. Once I got my nose into things, it dawned on me like a ton of bricks that the business was taking a real nosedive. Not only that, but my nose was itchy. We were sitting on the edge of disaster in a sink-or-swim situation, and that was just the first of many aqueous metaphors yet to come. I asked my assistant if he had a minute to discuss the matter, and he popped in for a second. Somewhere, fifty-nine seconds had been lost.

When I informed him that the business was going downhill, he offered to take a stab at the situation. This seemed perfectly appropriate, as he was brandishing an Exacto knife at the time. Conceding that I was in the dark about what to do, I asked him to shed some light on the matter. So he turned the lamp switch on. Brilliant idea.

I then shot off to a meeting, where the financial director got on my back about reduced profits. This was a crushing blow, and it didn't do much for my posture either. Back on my own turf in my office, I tried to touch base with the production manager. Getting in touch with her was difficult, and we ended up playing telephone tag. Unfortunately, no touchbacks were allowed.

After an eternity, we were finally able to get our heads together. This was a somewhat difficult maneuver, considering we were on the phone at the time. She wanted to chew the fat, so I suggested she try the Swiss steak, today's cafeteria special. She decided to sit on the problem until it blew over, but I insisted we tackle it head on from all sides. We were getting squeezed on our costs, but our bottom-line commitments had already been locked in. To make matters worse, someone had lost the key.

I passed the buck to my assistant, since I owed him for coffee anyway. The project was now on his plate and I gave him the green light to fork out some dollars to get a handle on the situation and get the ball rolling. He seemed to be on the ball, a practice he had learned from his days as a circus performer.

We threw some ideas back and forth and one of them knocked over a plant in the corner. After a while our impromptu blue sky session generated a whole flock of pie-in-the-sky alternatives. However, I suggested that a down-to-earth solution would be more appropriate, and just what the doctor ordered. Actually he only came in on alternate Tuesdays, but I'm certain he would have ordered it anyway.

We considered jacking up the price, blowing through a promotion offer, pumping out some inventory and firing up the sales force. Any of these would cost a bundle, but we couldn't afford to pull the plug on our sales, or the water cooler, for that matter. I was beating my head against the wall. A few minutes later someone from maintenance came by to patch up the considerable hole I had created.

Up to my ears in work, it was time to take a breather. So I headed down to the cafeteria, where I ran into the research analyst. As we were recovering from the collision, I made her aware of my predicament. Unfortunately, she couldn't help; her hands were tied after she had been tied up in a meeting.

Upon returning to my office, my boss paid me a call. It was a good thing he did because he owed me for coffee too. He had a beef with me and flew off the handle with some off-the-cuff remarks about a write-off, claiming I had been goofing off. Before he could lay off, I laid it on the line for him. Our new initiatives had slipped through the cracks and the competition was beating us to the punch. We would have to get ourselves out of the tangle and fix the problem, or we'd be in a real fix down the road. I got out a screwdriver, just in case.

It was time to bounce a couple of my ideas off the boss. He picked one up off the floor and tossed it back into my court, saying that he would be sold on the concept if it had more meat on it. There was a skeleton of an idea but it needed fleshing out, unlike the boss, who was twenty pounds overweight.

Later, my assistant and I thought we had the problem licked. But my boss jumped out of the boat, leaving us high and dry, up the creek without a paddle. It looked like our idea had been blown out of the water. We needed something to bail us out. So I grabbed a used coffee cup and began scooping up the ever increasing flood of metaphors that had filled my office.

Coffee cup in hand, I realized we had to do something to keep the ball rolling. So my assistant suggested another circus trick. It was time to put another idea on the table, but my boss said the proposal just wouldn't cut it. No wonder. The table was made of metal. If we were going to rally back with a counterattack, we would have to gather our forces and strike while the iron was hot. It had been set at delicate linens.

Finally an idea hit me. Ouch. The solution had been staring

me in the face all the time. So I stared back. This was tough, though, because I couldn't see the forest for the trees. All the time we had been barking up the wrong tree and going out on a limb when the solution was a grassroots idea that was within our grasp. Sort of like cheap bananas.

It seemed the new concept would hold water, so I decided to test the waters to see if the idea would float with my manager. I brought along a life jacket, just in case.

Out in the hallway we flagged down the president. We ran our idea up the flagpole with him, but he raised a red flag. This wasn't the time for flag waving, though, and for a moment it looked like we would fall out of bed, flag held patriotically in hand.

Nonetheless, we had already geared up for his comments and managed to pull it all together. The president said he would buy into the plan, but was a bit short of cash. So someone lent him a dollar. When the production manager caught wind of the proposal, he too jumped on the bandwagon. In fact, this was the most exercise he had had since jumping to a conclusion earlier in the week.

So that was it. We had found the solution to our business dilemma. At the end of the day, I was ready to pack it in and wrap it up. I just hoped the post office would deliver it on time.

**Metaphorically speaking, hit the nail on the head,
Cut the cliches, you can put them to bed.**

PLAN YOUR DAY

Even if you are on the right track – you'll get run over if you just sit there. Arthur Godfrey

---

The first three steps to effective planning are establishing your goals, determining your strategies and creating a master project list. Only then should you develop itemized day-to-day activities. They're more short term and more specific than the items you put on your project list.

Write a To Do List

Set aside the same time every day to plan your daily activities. Choose a quiet time when you can review past accomplishments, as well as future things to do. Then write down your list of top-priority activities that relate to your overall project list. Remember, project lists are main priorities you want to accomplish over the medium term. To-do lists are today's activities that will allow you to successfully complete each of your projects. Include specific activities, such as "Prepare exhibits for monthly report," rather than vague tasks such as "Work on report." Then, when you've completed an item, check it off. Doing this gives you a sense of accomplishment, even for small tasks.

Prioritize

Next, separate your to-do list into A, B and C priorities. A priorities are important to your long-term success. They are urgent and important. Finishing a new marketing plan or repairing a leaky roof is an A priority. B priorities may be urgent but not as important or they may be important, but not urgent. For instance, preparing the agenda for a meeting in a week's time is a B priority. C activities are those that would be nice to do if you get the time. Reading a trade magazine fits into this category. C priorities are neither urgent nor important. If everything looks like an A, go through your list again and separate items into A1, A2 and so on.

Block Your Time

Once you've created your list of things to do, block off time in your planner to work on them. Set aside chunks of time for specific high-priority activities. Choose times when others are least likely to interrupt you if you're working on your own. Choose times when you are most likely to reach others, if you're doing telephone work.

Then it's time to start by working on your A items. They should always come first. Don't work on a C just because it's easy to do. And if you find your A tasks are overwhelming, or if you don't think you have enough time to do anything on an A priority, the activity is too broad. Break your A priorities into small manageable chunks, so they're easy to accomplish. Even with just five minutes left before lunch or before an appointment, you should be able to make some progress on an A priority.

When you block your time, try to prevent interruptions from taking place. Put your phone on voice mail. Close your door. Don't schedule meetings for this time. If you need to, go to a quiet area, such as a boardroom, to do your work. When you block off time in your planner, you're making an appointment with yourself. If someone wants to meet you during that time, say "I'm sorry, I already have an appointment." But don't jam your day full of activities. Leave time for emergencies, special opportunities and thinking time.

Use Your Time Planner

As discussed in the previous chapter, use a time planner to keep track of your appointments. Use one only. Separate business and personal planners create confusion.

Always plan your time to achieve balance; don't forget to include family, fitness, recreation, social and spiritual activities.

Put a dollar value on each hour of your time and ask yourself whether someone else should be doing a task, or whether it should be done at all.

Be your own manager. Ask yourself if you have met your goals and what changes you must make to achieve them.

Do it now. People often will say, "Call me next week, and we'll book an appointment then." Respond by saying, "Let's save ourselves a call and do it now." Then write the appointment in your planner, including the street address and the person's phone number for handy reference.

Bunching Tasks

Bunching tasks together can save time. For instance, ask others to "save up" their interruptions or questions, and do the same for them. Go to your boss or your subordinate with a list of issues to discuss, rather than with one issue at a time. Avoid multiple trips to the copier or fax machine. Accumulate items in a folder on your desk and handle them all at once. Cluster tasks together, such as writing checks. Save social conversation with fellow employees until breaks or lunch.

Complete tasks as much as you can. Ask yourself, "Am I finished with this yet?" before moving on to something else. Break large projects into small pieces. When you are legitimately inter-rupted, mark the place in your work where you left off. For instance, a big time waster is having to start a data entry process over because you're not sure how far you got before you took a break or were interrupted.

TIME TRIVIA

The typical office worker only spends half of the time on A and B priorities combined. This consists of 30% of the time on A priorities and 20% on B pri-orities. But top performers spend more time on their A priorities, up to 40%. So the difference between average performance and great perfor-mance is just one extra hour per day spent on the things that really count.
PACE PRODUCTIVITY RESEARCH

The Story
That Never Began

B efore we begin this story, perhaps we should go back to the beginning: birth. Sylvia Slattery's entry into this world was certainly not without incident. In fact, it was quite a dilly.

Prior to the long-anticipated event, the as-yet-unnamed Sylvia had become quite accustomed to the warm, cozy environment inside her mother's womb. She really wasn't in a hurry to leave. Someday soon, she would get around to it. Meanwhile, she spent many a happy hour kicking the inside of her comfortable nesting place and planning a few changes to the upholstery. The color scheme just didn't work. And those walls would have to go.

Eventually Sylvia was born. Her arrival, about three weeks overdue, was a taste of many things to come. Perhaps it was an omen that the onslaught of her mother's labor had coincided with the return of an overdue library book, Stephen Hawking's *A Brief History of Time*.

While an infant, Sylvia quickly learned the art of procrastination. Oddly timed feeding sessions were not just a daily habit, they became an obsession. Just as mom was ready, Sylvia wasn't. Sylvia preferred to gurgle incoherently—the sort of behavior normally associated with city councillors.

A few years later, on the first day of kindergarten, Sylvia waited until the second day to show up.

Show-and-Tell sessions proved an exemplary introduction to the fine art of excuse making. One day when it was Sylvia's turn, she got up empty handed and recited a lengthy apology that displayed a level of intelligence and obfuscation well beyond her years: "With regard to the subject at hand, the aforementioned demonstration of personal artifacts, a temporary deferral is requested until a full and complete presentation is available..." Subjected to this speech, some of the kids screwed up their faces in revulsion, as if they were being offered a bowl of cold rice pudding tainted with Brussels sprouts and chicken liver. Most of them just took a nap. Sylvia's loquacious style was to haunt her on a fateful November day years later, but more about that later.

In grade nine, Sylvia developed a new series of excuses for failing to complete projects on time. By then her teachers learned that her mother had died six times, her house had burned down on three different occasions, she had been through fourteen different grandparents and her pet dog was run over on a monthly basis. Sylvia's penchant for exaggeration once got her caught. The dog gave it away.

Of course, when she grew up, Sylvia's problems were of a quite different nature, but more about those later.

University life presented a whole new set of deadlines and, thus, ever more elaborate excuses for not meeting them. She was known to hand in essays at 7:00 a.m. which were due the day before. She would slip them under a professor's door, with a pre-dated note. One time, a professor who got wise to her methods called her to assign a mid-term report. "OK Sylvia, I'm assigning you 'The Effect of Yodeling on Eighteenth-Century Scandinavian Pottery Making: A Comparative Analysis.' Please call me if you have any questions. And by the way, it's due yesterday."

Without even thinking, Sylvia asked, "Can I get a two-week extension?"

"Oh, I suppose," answered the all-too-wise professor. "I'll see you two weeks from yesterday then."

Certain events in one's life mark a turning point. These significant occasions change us from the way we were to the way we are: the first kiss, graduation from high school, becoming engaged. For Sylvia, it was the discovery of postdated checks.

But that was surpassed by another event of monumental importance. Halfway through her last semester at university, she burst into her roommate's room. It was a roomy room, exactly the sort of room a roommate would normally room in. Sylvia had a look of ecstasy on her face. "Guess what?" she exclaimed.

Ignazia, who had been sleeping, feigned enthusiasm. "A new boyfriend? You got an A on that yodeling thing?"

"No, silly! I just found out you can buy stuff now and pay later! Isn't that amazing?" The world had rarely seen better days.

Later that year, Sylvia became a charter member of the Last Minute Club. And it was no surprise that her favorite song was 'Tomorrow,' her favorite mini-series was The Day After and her favorite play was Same Time Next Year.

Some people set their watches ahead to make sure they're not late. Sylvia set her calendar ahead, though not always to great success. As a result, she once celebrated Christmas in late February.

When she reached adulthood, Sylvia refined the art of keeping up with yesterday. Her idea of a pleasant Saturday morning took place on Sunday afternoon, sitting on the front porch she hadn't got around to repairing, sipping warmed-over coffee from the day before, reading the previous Sunday's New York Times.

But her dilatory tactics eventually would come back to haunt her. The details can now be revealed. It was a usual day at the office, as Sylvia spent the early part of the morning starting to catch up on various tasks she had put off from the day before. As she was reading her mail, a sudden revelation of grave importance was revealed to her, as revelations normally are. Unfortunately, space is limited and so details cannot be provided. Suffice to say that whatever it was would just have to wait for another day.

Procrastination will mean a delay,
So why not commit to get started today?

STOP PROCRASTINATING

> *Procrastination is the art of keeping up with yesterday.* DON MARQUIS

Procrastination is fostered by habit. So to stop procrastinating you'll have to develop some new habits. But first, try to understand the causes for your procrastination. If you can, you're halfway there.

Procrastination can result from an apparently unpleasant task, a difficult and complex project, indecision, fear of failure (or, for that matter, fear of success) or a desire for perfection. In some cases, you may simply lack interest in the work, or you may foster some hostility towards the person who assigned the project. Recognize the difference between an appropriate decision to delay and an irrational postponement without justification.

Overcome procrastination by working on how you handle tasks and by creating an environment where distractions are minimized.

Task Strategies

- Clarify exactly what the task is. Perhaps it's not as complex as you had thought, or perhaps it's not needed at the level of detail you expected.
- Complete unpleasant tasks first. Schedule them for early in the day. .

- Reward yourself for accomplishments. Go out for special lunches when major projects are completed. If you haven't earned the reward, don't take it.
- Break large jobs into smaller, more manageable tasks.
- Plan and complete a start-up task, no matter how small.
- Set deadlines for yourself.
- Tell other people your deadlines and encourage them to check up on you.
- Focus on the end result, not just on the process.
- Develop a clear mental picture of the completed task and how good you will feel when it's finished.
- Make a game out of unpleasant tasks. Give yourself points, or conduct a running commentary on yourself as you do the task.

Environment Strategies

The other way to reduce opportunities for procrastination is to tailor your environment for work. Remove distractions such as water coolers, snacks, in-boxes, coffee machines and magazine racks. If you work at home, treat your office as an office. Don't go out to lunch before lunch time or watch television before the end of the day. Tell your family that you are not to be disturbed in your home office.

Finally, clear your desk of distracting items. Regularly file inactive items. Put away supplies and get rid of your mail. Often the waste basket is the best place for it.

TIME TRIVIA

For essential child-care responsibilities, such as bathing, feeding, reading and playing, parents' time is scarce. Employed women only spend 6.6 hours per week in undivided child care. Employed men only spend 2.5 hours per week on the same activities. Among unemployed parents, women spend additional time on child care, 12.9 hours per week. But unemployed men spend about the same time as employed men, only 2.6 hours per week.

TIME FOR LIFE, PENN STATE UNIVERSITY PRESS,
AS REPORTED IN NEWSWEEK

Hard work is often the easy work you did not do at the proper time. BERNARD MELTZER

Today is the tomorrow you worried about yesterday. ANONYMOUS

51

MANAGING OTHERS

The best executive is the one who has sense enough to pick good men to do what he wants done and self-restraint enough to keep from meddling with them while they do it.

THEODORE ROOSEVELT

Aliens Have Landed and They've Ruined the Grass

I first saw the aliens' landing spot when the snow melted. There it was, the impression of a perfect circle smack dab in the middle of my backyard. Evidently, a few wayward creatures from another planet had rudely plunked their vehicle down, thus creating a large, yellow impression in the middle of an otherwise green lawn. It was about twenty feet in diameter—not the mark of a particularly huge spaceship, but then aliens aren't all that large, are they?

The circle was nestled between the oak tree and a rusty garden set that had seen better days. I stared at the spot from an upstairs window for a few minutes. I had recently purchased the house, and no one had warned me of any previous intergalactic visits from inconsiderate aliens.

I imagined squat creatures with green skin, uncommonly large ears and a less-than-perfect knowledge of etiquette. They had probably arrived in the dead of night to investigate earthly vegetation, categorize life forms and pick up some discount store flyers.

I made my way downstairs and out to the lawn to examine the landing spot up close. On my way, I noticed my neighbor Alastair Beadle doing some weeding. I approached the fence dividing our properties. I leaned across and asked in a hushed tone, "Have we had any nocturnal excursions?"

"Are you talking dirty?" he asked.

"No, excursions, not the other thing. You know, alien land-ings," I practically whispered.

"Aliens?" Alastair responded, with a look of bewilderment bordering on disbelief. "What are you talking about? Did I miss something? Hey honey…" he began calling to his wife.

I interrupted him and showed him the round spot on the grass. He began laughing with spasmodic convulsions. "That's not a landing spot, that's where the previous owner had one of those above-ground pools."

"No. Really? Oh," I responded sheepishly. "Well, whatever it was, I have to fix that grass," I said, mortified. "What do I do, pour on some nitroglycerin?"

"You want the grass to grow up, not blow up," Alastair answered. "It's nitrogen you're thinking of. That's what grass needs, along with a bit of phosphorous and a dash of potash. Nitrogen promotes foliage growth and color. Phosphorous is essential to healthy root growth, but if you put too much on it will encourage clover. Potash keeps the grass healthy and green. Those numbers on the fertilizer packages usually show the per-centage of each of these three main nutrients in the mix. Now, the correct ratio…"

At this point I started to fade out, as he proceeded to give me a fifteen-minute chemistry lesson. He interspersed this lecture with a few nasty jabs at the previous owner of my house, who appar-ently had once attempted windsurfing in the above-ground pool.

Two weeks later, after stocking up on all of his recommended chemical demons, I was ready to apply a dry fertilizer mix, using my new hand-held spreader with its built-in crank. Alastair yelled a series of staccato instructions over the fence.

"Best time to fertilize is in the morning," he said authorita-tively, "after the dew evaporates. And wear your spiked golf shoes when your apply it…that way the fertilizer gets where it belongs quicker." He continued his advice in note form. "Make sure to water. Won't be rain for a couple of days. Grass will burn if the fertilizer doesn't soak in. Never at night. Pros will tell ya, damp grass—welcome wagon for bugs and disease."

He then assumed the role of mission control, providing detailed course corrections as I applied the mix. "Go left, forward a bit, just a touch more there, that's it, keep it up…"

Two weeks later I arose early one morning to admire my handiwork. The circle had faded and the grass was a bright green. I wandered over to the garden and began peacefully puttering through the petunias, when I spotted a gold plaque half buried in the dirt. As I approached, it began to emit a faint glow. It was about nine inches long, four inches wide and one inch deep (perhaps slightly more in metric). Was it a child's toy? A lost treasure?

Then I noticed a series of tiny inscriptions embossed on one side. There were dozens of lines of script in a multitude of foreign languages. I recognized only the English and French versions. Just a few simple words in tiny letters: "We came in peace. Sorry about the grass."

Advisors you choose can help you along,
Interference is short and advice should be long.

BUILD A PERSONAL SUCCESS TEAM

Too bad that all the people who know how to run the country are busy driving taxicabs and cutting hair. **George Burns**

Everyone likes to give advice, whether it's a co-worker or your neighbor. But wisdom is as important as advice, and when you find people who can provide you with both, make them part of your team. Whether you're a manager, an entrepreneur or a stay-at-home parent, the team you recruit to help can make a major difference to your success. The key is to find those who have already been there. Friends and neighbors may like to give you their perspective, but professionals who have been through the process before can provide the insights you need, not just the advice you'll shun.

When recruiting your team, pay people to do the things you can't do yourself or don't like doing, such as:
• Legal work
• Bookkeeping and accounting
• Computer repairs
• Software programming
• Deliveries
• Graphic design
• Public relations

Pay your suppliers of professional services what they want. Don't haggle over prices, even though you could probably talk them into reducing their fees by 10 percent. Instead, create good relationships so they will enjoy working with you and consider themselves part of your team. With a good relationship, they're likely to give you service value that's worth 20 percent more than what you pay. That's good math, as well as good business.

If you're an entrepreneur, create a board of advisors. They don't need to have the formal responsibilities of a board of directors, and don't need to meet each other. They are simply professionals who take an interest in your business and who want to see you succeed. You can meet them every quarter to get their advice and to ensure you're staying on track. Or you may decide not to create a formal arrangement at all. But stay in touch with them.

In between formal meetings, keep your directors or advisors regularly informed. Send them newsletters and other updates. When you call them, ask for their advice and thank them when you've followed it, describing what the results were.

Finally, take successful business people out to lunch occasionally and ask for tips on achieving peak performance. They've seen it all, and they'll show you the way.

TIME TRIVIA

According to the Guinness Book of World Records, the longest measure of time is the kalpa in Hindu chronology. It is equivalent to 4,320 million years. On the other hand, according to people who live in New York City, the shortest possible unit of time is the nanosecond. It is the time between when the light turns green and the cab driver behind you honks his horn.

The Tale of the Bent Pole

The last time I arranged a big financing deal was when I discovered my credit card was over the limit at the local pizza joint.

So I found myself slightly squeamish when a potential buyer, the person to whom we might entrust the future of our house, pulled down his horn-rimmed glasses, glowered at me and asked, somewhat cautiously, "I presume you're prepared to arrange a vendor take back?" This question perplexed me. I was trying to sell the house, not take it back. At that precise moment, I realized I was in trouble.

Flower arranging I could handle. Mortgage arranging was something else. Mr. Horn-Rimmed Glasses did not buy.

It had all started one rainy autumn day when I decided the house just wasn't big enough for both of us. One of us had to go. The house decided to stay put.

"Time to move," I said to my wife, Beatrice.

"You just stand up and put one foot in front of the other," she said.

"No, I meant we should move somewhere else."

"OK. Try doing it in the living room."

"You know, I'll bet we could sell the house ourselves and save a bundle on commissions. We could put up a For Sale sign. There are always lots of people driving by. I see them taking pictures all the time."

"Drive-by shootings you mean," Beatrice said wryly.

Finding a For Sale sign was just the first of many subsequent calamities. It took three telephone calls, two trips to the shopping mall and a slightly misdirected fax that ended up somewhere in Africa. I finally found a sign, slightly torn, buried at the bottom of a pile of trilingual welcome mats at the hardware store.

The owner looked at me with a mischievous grin, "So, you're going it alone, huh? Humph, good luck." The "humph" part worried me, as did the somewhat mangled condition of the sign.

Later that day I walked out to the front lawn, mallet in one hand, battered sign in the other. I positioned the pole on the ground and gave it a good whack. This merely succeeded in bending the pole. The ground had frozen solid and was not particularly keen on having a rather blunt rod of flimsy steel smashed into it. However, with help from my trusty electric drill, I managed to create a modest hole. "Honey, would you mind moving it a bit closer towards the tree?" Beatrice asked when she saw it. I proceeded to carve out hole number two. Three drill bits and thirteen holes later, we finally agreed on a suitable spot.

Beatrice was in charge of printing the lower part of the sign. When she finished, I complimented her on her fine calligraphy, "It looks terrific, sweetie, but is it really necessary to say 'Let's make a deal' and 'The price is right'?" Visions of Monty Hall raced through my head. The gothic hand lettering on the modestly ripped sign, placed on the subtly bent pole in my somewhat crooked hole, gave the entire contrivance a tilted, tattered look.

Next we decided to place a newspaper ad in an attempt to attract buyers. I handled the writing this time, with input from my wife. "Beatrice, how about saying the house comes with a soothing atmospheric ambiance?"

"You mean the racket from the highway?" she answered.

"All right, well for the back room, should we say cozy den or intimate family space?"

"It's a mud room."

"Hmm. OK, how about pleasant wildlife nearby?"

"I don't think that's how you normally describe the raccoons in the attic."

I completed the ad and published it to no avail, wondering all along what an avail would look like if I happened to find one.

The aforementioned Mr. Horn-Rimmed Glasses had discovered the house by accident, only because he was involved in a local citizens' committee that was trying to clear up what he called "ambient, non-intrusive visual pollution." My For Sale sign had been tops on his list.

After he left, our neighbor Ridley Wantsall dropped by to offer a little friendly advice. Pipe in hand, he gazed at the ceiling, furrowed his brow and quietly but determinedly asked, "What do you think you'll get for it?" I told him our asking price. "Sounds about twenty G's low to me," he concluded. It seemed to me only bankers and gangsters ever used phrases like "twenty G's."

The selling price had been suggested to us by the uncle of a friend of a brother-in-law who happened to be in the business a few years ago and who had chatted with us briefly over the phone.

"The price is too low? So what do you suggest? I'm in a real dilemma," I said.

"A dilemma," Ridley said. "Edmund Volkart once defined a dilemma as any situation requiring a choice between disagreeable alternatives, such as voting, turning on the television set or selecting a dentist. You know, maybe you just need to delegate the sale of your house. It might be time to find a good real estate agent."

We found one, and within days he had conducted a market survey, provided an appraisal, arranged for photography, placed a multiple listing ad, organized an open house, contacted buyers and conducted three showings. The house was sold in ten days.

Despite his expertise, he had encountered just one small difficulty, which provided us with heart-warming consolation. It had something to do with a futile attempt to pound a sign into hole number fourteen.

Don't do a job that someone else could,
Delegate well to those who are good.

DELEGATE

Work is of two kinds: first, altering the position of matter at or near the earth's surface relative to other matter; second, telling other people to do so. BERTRAND RUSSELL

One definition of management is working through individuals and groups to accomplish organizational goals and objectives. To be an effective manager, you need to be skilled in planning, organizing, motivating and controlling. Delegation takes skill in all four areas. The assignment of tasks allows you to multiply your efforts through others.

Consider What Activities Should be Delegated

When considering what to delegate, first examine what you can eliminate. If you shouldn't be doing an activity, then perhaps you shouldn't be giving the activity away to others. Eliminate it.

There are some activities that cannot or should not be delegated. Anything related to employee feedback, for instance, can't be delegated. You can't ask someone else to conduct a performance review, provide discipline or fire an employee.

For other tasks you're considering delegating, ask yourself whether you'd be prepared to do it yourself. Have you done it in the past? This is a good test of whether it's appropriate to delegate something.

Though it may sound contradictory, you should, as a general rule, delegate the routine activities that you don't want to delegate. These include:
- Fact-finding assignments
- Preparation of rough drafts of reports
- Problem analysis and recommended actions
- Collection of data for reports
- Logistics booking (travel, meeting rooms, audio visual equipment)

Don't hold onto activities just because you like doing them, especially if they interfere with priority items. The sign of a poor manager is the statement, "I'm the only person who has the right skills or knowledge to do this properly." Managers who believe this are generally surprised at how much others will contribute when given an opportunity.

Assigning Tasks

Create a plan to delegate. Don't just give out assignments haphazardly. Examine your master project list first. If you weren't around, which projects would be done by someone else? Invest short-term time in training to gain a long-term increase in productivity. Watch out for another favorite phrase used by those who can't delegate: "By the time I showed someone else how to do it, I might as well have done it myself."

Delegation is an investment in your own future, as well as in your team's future. It takes time to prepare assignments, to communicate them to others and to train subordinates. But the long-term payoffs are better use of your time and a stronger organization.

Make sure that tasks are delegated to the right people and that you communicate often enough to know how the project is proceeding. Delegate, don't abdicate.

Working with Subordinates

The standards for successful completion of tasks must be clear.

It's your job to clearly identify the quality level, timelines and input from others required. It's the delegate's job to determine how to meet the standards. So delegate the objective, not the procedure. Outline the desired results, not the methodology. Your subordinates will find a way to achieve the objective, and they may end up doing a better job than you. Be prepared to trade short-term errors for long-term results.

Don't always give tasks to the strongest, most experienced or first available person. Development of people is one of the goals of delegation. Explain the benefits for those who will be accepting assignments. They may be looking for broader exposure, prestige, an opportunity to contribute new ideas or a chance to learn a new skill along the way. By spread delegation around, you give people new experiences as part of their training.

Be sure to delegate the authority along with the responsibility. Trust people to do well, and don't look over their shoulders or check up on them along the way, unless they ask you to do so. Remain accessible if they really need you.

Then reward people for successfully completing assignments through praise, announcements, newsletters or awards.

TIME TRIVIA

When asked, "What things, within your control, get in the way of your productivity?" the top five responses among office workers were:

1. Poor planning, time management or organizational skills
2. Paperwork and administrative tasks
3. Socializing and gossip
4. No focus, trying to do too many things at once
5. Internal communications

PACE PRODUCTIVITY RESEARCH

The Performance Review—
Next Contestant Please

Dean Hawkshaw looked up from his cubicle and saw his boss, Helga Dilworth, hovering nearby. It was rare that she visited him. Normally she called by phone, even though Dean's cubicle was right outside her office, within spitting distance of her own desk. Dean had checked once.

Helga had a booming voice, so loud that Dean would place the receiver on his desk when she called, using it as a makeshift speaker phone.

What she mastered in volume, she lacked in people skills. Helga was a twenty-year veteran of the department, which she ran coolly and efficiently. But she had a bad habit of mixing up her employees' names.

"Uh, Don, the company wants me to do a performance review on you. Could you drop by my office at 2 p.m. this afternoon?" she boomed.

"Sure, but it's Dean. Should I prepare something?"

"Oh, no. I'm certain we can do it pretty quickly. You know, just fill out the forms and all. They're due tomorrow," she answered.

She returned to her office, and Dean scratched his head. Later that afternoon he entered her office and sat down.

"OK, Dunne, I'd say your performance on the Database Rectification Assembly Team has been pretty good."

"DRAT you mean. Actually, I wasn't on that team," said Dean. "And it's Dean."

"Oh? You weren't? Oh, yes." She shuffled through a pile of file folders. "Wait a minute. That's right, you're the..." Just then, her phone rang. "Helga Dilworth speaking," she answered. She paused as she listened, then spoke to the caller in a voice like a foghorn that could raise the dead. "Well, I'd say the new conditioners are relatively atypical in the vast majority..." She droned on like a buzz saw.

Meanwhile, Dean sat gazing about the room. In one corner a plant grew an inch as he listened to Helga prattling away. Finally she hung up the phone and looked at Dean. "OK, where were we, Dan?"

"Dean."

"Yes, sorry, Dean. Dean," she said, slapping her head in frustration. Dean wondered whether the head slapping was meant to make her brain work better, sort of like kicking an ailing photocopier. "It says here I'm supposed to talk to you about needs for improvement."

"Yes, that's right."

"Well, let's see. Do you think you need a new plant, would that be of use?"

"Yes, though I think they were referring to improving my skills, not the decor. Actually I wanted to improve my negotiating techniques. Could I get a hundred-dollar credit for a course I'd like to take?"

"I'm not sure if it's in the budget right now. How would two hundred dollars sound?"

"Well I suppose I could settle for seventy-five dollars."

"I'm sorry. Two hundred and fifty dollars is my last offer."

"Uh, yup, I suppose," said Dean, a bit befuddled.

"Sold then, for two twenty. OK, well I'll type this up. I think we'll give you a satisfactory plus, that sounds pretty good, doesn't it? And are you supposed to get a raise? I could get one for you, perhaps."

"Actually, it's automatic in two months' time, as per our union's collective agreement. But thank you, anyway."

Dean returned to his desk, mildly confident that Helga still approved of his results and that he still had his job. He watched as his comrade Jeremy headed into her office.

"Hello, Jerry," he heard as the door closed.

Performance reviews should be done now and then,
To counsel and guide and plan once again.

CONDUCT A
PERFORMANCE APPRAISAL

---

*A good manager knows that there is more
than one way to skin a cat. A great manager can
convince the cat that it is necessary.* GENE PERRET

The purpose of a performance appraisal is to document behavior so that decisions about assignments, training, promotions or salary can be justified. Mostly though, the appraisal is designed to improve the performance of those being reviewed. It is a formal procedure based on input from both the manager and the employee which is prepared in advance.

Giving a performance appraisal can be a worthwhile and necessary investment. It will save you day-to-day supervision time and result in better performance from your employees down the road.

Before the Review

Ensure that the necessary data are available in advance. This data will include project lists, reports, letters of commendation, the previous appraisal and the actual job description. Then inform the employee of the date for the review. Set aside uninterrupted time, usually forty-five minutes to an hour. Ask the employee to prepare by writing out a self-assessment.

During the Review

Put the other person at ease. Early on, explain the purpose of the performance appraisal again. Control the pace and direction of the interview. Solicit employee input of his or her own performance. Ask an easy question such as, "Tell me how you feel you've been doing." Or, "How would you sum up your accomplishments in the last six months?" Use active listening to make sure you understand. Encourage employees to be self-critical. Ask, "Where do you think you could improve?"

Then convey your own systematic appraisal based on facts, performance and behaviors observed, not on inference and personality. Avoid conjectures about motivations or a discussion of personality. Employees' attitudes can't be changed as easily as actions can. Beware of judgmental words such as lazy, uncaring, stupid, self-centered and pompous, unless you're quoting frequent comments from other people. Also, make sure the employee understands how you are defining terms. Words such as thorough, good, cooperative and disruptive can be defined in too many ways. When you say the employee has good results, do you mean that the results are only acceptable, or that you are genuinely pleased with them?

Compare performance versus established standards, previous appraisals and expectations. Clearly identify the gap between where employees are and where they should be. Take the time to document and substantiate poor performance, as well as outstanding achievements.

Clarify your ratings system and make sure that it means the same thing to the employee as it does to you. Many organizations use standard forms. Do you understand what the different sections mean? What would someone have to do to reach a maximum possible rating?

After the Appraisal

When you've provided an assessment, ensure that your employee understands what you've said. Then build coaching and counseling into the discussion. Prepare a plan for future action. Identify training plans and new goals, as well as expected results.

Conclude on a positive note, with a clear understanding of next steps by both parties. Then, follow up with a written summary or agreement by one or both parties. In the weeks after the review, follow through on the commitments you made towards training, the work environment or projects.

Separate discussions about merit pay increases from the performance discussion. The objective is to coach and to counsel. Salary should be handled at a different time so that the employee will not see performance as the primary factor affecting salary.

Do Not:
- Get into conflicts or arguments.
- Suggest resolution through a boss or third party.
- Talk too much.
- Jump to conclusions—hear the employee's side first.
- Blame others who aren't present or allow the employee to blame others.
- Make promises that can't be kept by either party.
- Be interrupted by distractions. Make sure your calls are being handled by someone else or by voice mail.

TIME TRIVIA

Personal training doesn't take up much time in the typical office worker's life. Among those who measured it, training adds up to only 50 minutes per week, essentially 2 sessions of about 25 minutes each. This is just under 2% of the overall work week.

PACE PRODUCTIVITY RESEARCH

RUNNING MEETINGS

Hardly anyone writes because you can't really write down all you know. And even if you do write, nobody will read it. So there are meetings, and meetings about meetings, and meetings to plan reports, and meetings to review the status of reports. And what these meetings are about is people just trying to figure out what they are doing. PAUL STRASSMANN, FORMER VICE PRESIDENT, XEROX

Mind if I Work while You Interrupt Me?

T he large gorilla in the doorway of Donelda Cahoon's office waved its arms frantically. Unaccustomed as she was to this sort of interruption, Donelda's first reaction was to scream. Office etiquette got the better of her and she considered calling building security instead. But they would take too long to arrive, and she felt pressed for time. So she blurted out her standard response to unexpected visitors: "Take a seat. May I help you? How about a coffee?"

The gorilla relaxed and sauntered in. A deep, muted voice made its way through the thick mask, "I'm really lost. I'm Arnold, I'm looking for Dan in Payroll. I'm his stag gift." Always helpful, Donelda escorted the gorilla on what turned out to be a fifteen-minute excursion to the payroll department, where the gorilla sang an off-key version of a decidedly off-color song.

Back at her desk, Donelda continued writing her feasibility report on the new E-Scential line of parsley-scented deodorants, to be packaged in ruddy brown containers that had an uncanny resemblance to bloated earthworms. Just as she was about to start summarizing the scathing responses to the packaging, Donelda was again interrupted, this time by Lividia, her secretary.

Although Lividia didn't look as threatening as the gorilla, she sounded much worse. Her distinctively irritating whine could wake corpses. "Donellldaaa," she whined, sounding like a CD skipping, "like, we've run out of staples, eh? Like, when can you authorize some new ones? Like, todaaay?" Fingernails scraping on a chalkboard were only slightly less aggravating. Donelda couldn't bear the thought of suffering through any further requests. So she consulted her catalog of office products, called the purchasing department, checked with office supplies, rechecked the catalog, filled out two forms and grew another gray hair. All for a two-dollar box of staples.

A few minutes later, another visitor appeared. It was Molly Mumby, a claims clerk whose job consisted of filing forms that most people had never heard of and wouldn't have known what to do with if they received one. Molly was on maternity leave and had brought her new baby for the usual round of gathering about to make silly infant noises. When three fellow staff members dropped into Donelda's office, their conversation quickly devolved from professional candor to infantile gibberish. "Cootchie coo" and "Ahhhh," the most popular expressions, were given an eerie twist by Lividia, whose baby talk sounded like a chain saw in a snit. Not without its heated moments, the discussion on whether the baby looked more like mom or dad was intense. It was like a debate on whether toilet roll sheets should hang from the inside or the outside. (It's the inside, by the way.)

As word quickly spread, more and more co-workers crowded into Donelda's small office, delighting at the cute baby. Cuteness took on the air of some exquisitely rare property that only this baby had been blessed with. Donelda wondered aloud who got all the ugly babies, in a feeble attempt to cause a scene and embarrass everyone out of her office. But Molly continued to relish the attention. She brought out the inevitable photos. Dozens of out-of-focus shots with cut-off heads generated sycophantic responses.

When the baby began to cry, Molly asked politely, "Could you clear some of these files off your credenza, Donelda, so I can change him? The little ducky wucky has just done a little, you know, number two jobby in his panty wanties." Someone would have to teach her real English. Donelda was enjoying the inconvenience about as much as root canal surgery.

When mother, baby, staff and the odor of baby poop eventually left the room, Donelda barricaded her office door to keep everyone out. Her makeshift rampart consisted of a waste basket decorated with happy face stickers, an unwanted lamp made from used exhaust pipes, an almost dead potted plant and a couple of soiled diapers. This would keep those pesky interruptions out, she thought. But once she finished her fortification, she realized it would be as difficult for her to get out as for others to get in.

Finally, in frustration, she went to Crispin Quirty for help. At his desk, he was busy building what looked like a small molecule made from paper clips. He stood up as Donelda walked in, and he pointed to his handiwork. "Do you like our new organizational model? A bit unstable perhaps, but then most of our senior executives are. Anyway, what can I do for you?"

Donelda sighed, "I can't stand all the constant interruptions I get. Have you got a minute to help?"

"Sure do. How about at two o'clock this afternoon? I'll drop by your office." Donelda left, amazed at how Quirty had neatly handled her interruption by delaying their meeting.

Promptly at two o'clock, Crispin Quirty visited Donelda in her office. He was carrying another contraption, a model of a popsicle stick made out of pieces of an old airplane. He remained standing as Donelda complimented him.

"I like the way you delayed our meeting. Have you got any other tricks?"

"Sure, have I shown you my disappearing rabbit? It was here a minute ago, now it's gone. Anyway, preventing walk-in visitors is really about establishing some procedures. Get your assistant to screen visitors before they get to you. In fact, from what I know of Lividia, she could scare most people away for good. Also, set a time limit at the beginning of informal meetings, and stick to it by making sure people see you looking at your watch. Another technique is to stand up when people walk into your office, so they don't get too comfortable. Or you can always leave things on your extra chairs so that visitors don't sit down."

"Like what, books?"

"Could do the trick. Or a briefcase, file folder, whoopee cushion, dead rat, sewage slime."

"Yucch, that's gross!"

"That's what the last person said when they saw old Buddy lying in my office. My pet slug. Former pet, I should say. Another strategy is to go somewhere else to get more concentration time. You won't get interrupted if you're not in your office. We have a great word for that."

"Hiding?"

Quirty nodded as she left. Donelda immediately began trying out his ideas. Later that week, she noticed a marked increase in her concentration time. That is, until her staff arrived the following week with a surprise birthday cake. "Can this wait until tomorrow?" Donelda joked as she blew out the candles.

Interruptions will cause you constant delay,
Keeping them short means saving your day.

HANDLE WALK-IN VISITORS

According to a recent issue of **Psychology Today,** *research shows that a slight protrusion of your tongue between your lips, while you're working, is taken as a tacit "Do Not Disturb" sign by most people. The next time you're trying to complete a file on an impossible task, you might want to try this technique.* Canadian Lawyer MAGAZINE

Unlike other time wasters, walk-in visitors are often out of your control. They come in when you least expect them, they talk more than you'd like, and they stay longer than they should. The key to interruptions, like other time management issues, is to regain control. You need not be at the mercy of interruptions if you plan well and if you have an arsenal of tactics at the ready when visitors become an imposition.

Create Isolation

The easiest way to prevent interruptions is to isolate yourself. Work in a conference room, close the door of your office or do important projects at home if necessary.

The next-best technique is to block your time. Establish a quiet hour to create essential private time. Inform co-workers that you like to come in at perhaps 8:00 a.m. and work on your own until 9:30

a.m. Only after that time should you schedule meetings. During your quiet time, handle larger, important projects first, before you read your mail and before interruptions are likely to occur.

Discourage Lingering

If you're fortunate enough to have a secretary or an assistant, allow him or her to screen visitors, based on clear guidelines as to what kinds of interruptions are appropriate. If the interruption can wait, the assistant should have the authority to schedule a subsequent meeting or should divert the inquiry to someone else.

But inevitably visitors will arrive. When someone walks into your office and you're really pressed for time, immediately stand up. That way, your visitor is less likely to sit down and get comfortable. Or you might ask visitors how long their requests will take. Then schedule a meeting by saying, "I'd like to talk to you about that. Can I come by your office in about five minutes?" This gives you more control.

Subordinates might tend to drop by numerous times throughout the day. Ask them to "save up" items of importance and deal with them in a bunch at an appointed time.

If they insist on a discussion right away, encourage them to get to the point quickly. Say, "Can you summarize the problem and what you'd like me to do about it in ten words or less?" Often, people will tell a story instead of present an issue.

If you've set a time limit, check your watch. Do it in an obvious way and make sure to announce the end of the allotted time when it comes.

Extreme Measures

Some time management experts suggest more unconventional measures. For instance, you could temporarily place a binder or a briefcase on the extra chair in your office to discourage others from sitting down.

When visitors linger, invent a meeting that you have to go to, or confess that you promised to call someone back about a confidential matter at exactly this time. This tactic may not be entirely ethical, but it may be necessary in an awkward situation. Another technique is to go to another area to do a task such as photocopying or faxing. Ask the visitor along, but once there, bring closure to the conversation and leave the person there. Chances are he or she won't come back to your office with you.

Don't let your own strategy become counterproductive to the organization. What may benefit you as an individual may be detrimental to the team. Keeping your door closed will result in greater concentration, but it might frustrate your colleagues, as they could waste their own time because you weren't available for help.

TIME TRIVIA

The fastest reproductive cycle of human body cells occurs in the rectum, where cells divide every 13 hours. The longest cycle is that of body hair, excluding the scalp, which takes 5.5 months for renewal.

PAUL RICE, TIMESOURCE

Let's Vote on Whether to Vote

Felicia Fetherstonhaugh was dreading the weekly meeting of the Pennies for Penelope the Penguin Committee. Something deep inside warned her that, just like last week's meeting, this one would run with the all of the finesse of a drunken cyclist doing figure eights on a skating rink. While blindfolded. But Felicia had committed herself to help with her community group's newest project, and she didn't want to back out.

She arrived at chairman Sydney Hackenberger's house precisely at the designated 6:15 p.m. start time. No one else had showed up yet. She waited impatiently, while reading an old, dog-eared copy of *National Enquirer*. Apparently, Elvis had kidnapped some aliens and was teaching them to play guitar.

At 6:30 p.m. Sydney proclaimed to those present that the turnout was "quite good." Besides Felicia, the turnout consisted of Sydney, his wife Blossom, who was in the kitchen burning popcorn, Sydney's dog (Rufus the Monster) and his four-year-old daughter, who kept trying to give Felicia an unwanted manicure. While waiting for the others to arrive, Sidney proudly announced that this would be a special meeting. Two types of coffee were being served. He then reviewed the purpose of the project: to raise money for Penelope, a trained penguin at the local zoo who had hurt a flipper during a recent performance.

At 6:45 p.m. Anthony Slobodsky and his girlfriend, Ignazia Grunwald, arrived. They had been held up on the highway after a truck filled with fluorescent ping-pong balls had spilled its load. At 7:10 p.m. Gerald McGuckin appeared. He claimed to be early because, according to his notes, the meeting was to start at 7:15 p.m. For the next fifteen minutes, the committee members munched on cold, burnt popcorn while trying to decide on a date for the following meeting.

When the meeting finally started, Felicia asked Sydney for an agenda. "Agenda?" Sydney answered. "Yeah, well, I've got it all in my head, so we don't really need one." A heated discussion then ensued on whether to first discuss the fund-raising event, which was to be a sleep-a-thon, or the wrap-up party for the volunteers.

Felicia then asked to review the minutes from the previous meeting. Unfortunately, after much fruitless scrounging around, Gerald remembered that the minutes had been lost down a sewer grate on the way to a post-meeting rendezvous at a local bar. Felicia suggested that they look at the minutes from the prior meeting to the last. After another flurry of scrounging around, Gerald found them scribbled on the inside back cover of a slightly ragged and thoroughly trashy spy novel. The good news was that the minutes contained the names of some potential sponsors. The bad news was that Gerald couldn't determine which of the hastily scrawled names referred to the sponsors and which referred to the stockbroker whom he had been flirting with in the bar.

The discussions continued, although without Gerald, who, exhausted from all of his scrounging, had taken to idly reading the newspaper. Suddenly, he spotted an article in the local news section, slapped his hand to his forehead in astonishment and jumped to his feet. "Oh my god, guess what? This is astonishing. Incredible!" he exclaimed with all of the profundity associated with the announcement of an imminent nuclear attack. "Penelope has recovered from her wound."

"Well, then, I guess we should disband the committee," announced Felicia.

"No way!" retorted Sydney. "Our committee was promised money to get this going and we're going to spend all of it."

Felicia interjected, "I thought the purpose of the project was to raise money."

"Sure, but you have to spend money to raise money," responded Sydney. "Postage, letterhead, the planning party, the after party, gifts for each of the donors, an embossed plaque for the penguin house..." The list went on.

The group spent the next twenty minutes deciding what to order for dinner. They decided on pizza and went on to debate what size, what toppings and even from what outlet to order from. Sydney instituted strict parliamentary procedure. Motions were followed by amendments, revisions, counterarguments, points of order and points of privilege. As the committee debated how to extricate itself from a tangled web of procedural mish mash, Anthony made a definitive proposal. "I suggest we vote on whether to take a vote." They ended up ordering chicken.

After waiting for, consuming and cleaning up after the chicken, the meeting finally resumed. Felicia interjected, "We seem to be spending an awful lot of time on this, and we're not really getting anywhere. We've got an idea, but no goals, no plans and no commitments." She then outlined some techniques to improve the meeting dynamics, including starting on time, sticking to the agenda, appointing a chairperson and having only one person speak at a time.

As a result, the next meeting ran much more smoothly. The group decided to hold the sleep-a-thon in the city's main square on a Saturday night in November. Television coverage would help publicize the event between periods during a hockey broadcast. Participants would sleep on inflatable rubber mattresses, floating on a large, portable swimming pool. With new-age music playing in the background and Penelope swimming around the sleeping bodies, it would be like a surreal update of an Esther Williams extravaganza.

But troublesome questions remained. Would participants be allowed breaks, or would continuous sleeping be required? Would couples be allowed? What if the water in the swimming pool froze?

And the most troublesome question of all: What would happen to the proceeds of the event now that Penelope had healed? When the subject arose, Sydney stood up and proudly addressed the assembled multitude of four.

"I've decided to continue with another zoological undertaking. As of now, we will now embark with energy, gusto, enthusiasm and other synonyms to raise money for a new cause: Dollars for Dentures for Delores the Donkey!"

Preparing agendas will keep you on track,
At all of your meetings, you'll soon get the knack.

PREPARE FOR MEETINGS

Perhaps Hell is nothing more than an enormous conference of those who, with little or nothing to say, take an eternity to say it. DUDLEY C. STONE

Do you dislike going to meetings? It's ironic that despite the pleasant social interaction at meetings, many people consider them a waste of time.

As the chairperson, preparing an agenda in advance helps you determine which items you want to cover. You can also use the agenda to communicate to participants what they will be considering and what is expected of them. An agenda helps create order and control at the meeting. Ideally, attenders should have a copy in advance.

Establish an Agenda

If someone else is preparing the agenda, approach that person beforehand to make sure your items are on the list for discussion.

The most important item on the agenda is the purpose of the meeting. You should be able to state it in one succinct sentence, such as, "To review and approve details of the annual budget." Keep the list of items to be covered specific and focused. What do you expect to happen after each item is finished? You should also include the time, the place, the names of those who will be attending and the start and end times. End times are rarely given, but people are impressed when during the meeting, you count down the time remaining and then adjourn on time. Always start and finish with positive items.

Consider starting meetings at oddball times, such as 10:08 a.m. If you want a short meeting, schedule it for late in the day. Business has a tendency to move quickly as it approaches five o'clock.

Make a formal invitation, usually in person or by telephone at least a week in advance. Send a follow-up confirmation note and the agenda after everyone's attendance has been confirmed. Then, try to remind those who will be attending. Have an assistant call to remind attendees about the meeting, or mention it to them yourself in conversation. Although it shouldn't be necessary, some people require confirmation that the meeting is still on. Somehow, they expect appointments to be broken. If you're unable to circulate an agenda in advance, write it on a flip chart or white board before participants arrive.

TIME TRIVIA

The average amount of time spent by office workers in meetings is 6½ hours per week per employee, or 14% of each employee's time. Among managers only, meetings take up 10 hours per week, or 19% of their time.

PACE PRODUCTIVITY RESEARCH

Chronicle of a Chronically Ill Meeting

Willard Thistlewaite's meeting invitation sounded urgent: "Bernice, we need you at our meeting on Monday. Can you come?"

"Well, I suppose," Bernice Crampsey answered reluctantly. She was worried that accepting the invitation might turn out to be a big mistake. "What's it about?"

"We have to have a meeting for the new products group."

"All right, so what's it about?" asked Bernice.

"Well, we've been asked to come up with a new product plan and we need you there."

"Yes, but what exactly will be happening at the meeting?"

"Well, key issues. You know, planning. It's important that the key people are there. We're trying to find the key to productivity."

"Maybe you need a locksmith. But seriously, am I really needed? You still haven't told me exactly what's going on at the meeting."

"Well…" began Willard.

Suddenly the phone rang. Bernice answered it. An internal auditor was inviting her to yet another meeting. As Bernice continued the phone call, she glanced up to see Willard waving at her. Willard pronounced a few words without making a sound.

Bernice didn't read lips and had no idea what he was saying. Willard scribbled in Bernice's appointment book, waved good-bye and left, as Bernice continued her phone conversation. Apparently, Bernice had been booked. She meant to call Willard back but never got around to it.

Two days later, Bernice sat in the conference room twiddling her thumbs. She began to tie them in a knot. She was waiting impatiently with four other managers for the meeting to begin.

Willard finally started. "I'm sure no one will mind if we start just a little bit late." Bernice considered this a bold assumption. Why did they always punish those who committed to being on time and reward those who were late?

So Bernice and the others resigned themselves to idle chit chat. Movies. Weather. Easy listening radio. What to do with soiled kitty litter. Willard got up a few minutes later and pronounced, "We'll begin in a minute." This was the second in a series of subtle incongruities. Four minutes later, nothing had happened.

Finally a few drifters wandered in. "Good morning ladies and gentlemen," said Willard. In fact, it had not been a very good morning. It had rained. "As you know, our main purpose today is to review the budget figures and to determine how to make the presentation to upper management." That was two main purposes, and counting.

"I'll try to get us out of here in an hour." Bernice reflected on how the phrase "I'll try" was one of the most redundant and useless in the English language. What if Willard didn't succeed? Would he have to stand in the corner or something?

"We're going to need an official chairman for the meeting," Willard said. Participants began to fidget nervously, anticipating a fait accompli, or some other handy French idiom. "Are there any volunteers?" Willard asked. He then waited for what he considered a reasonable length of time for a response—about one tenth of a millisecond. Willard continued, "If no one minds then, perhaps I'll act as chairman." Of course, everyone minded.

Willard then pronounced, "The production scheduling system is an a priori issue. We'll need an ad hoc committee to look at the issues, quid pro quo." Latin wasn't his strong suit. "I'm sure everyone would agree on the need for a quick fix." Actually, no one agreed. They weren't given much of a chance.

Willard continued, "Now, I'm not an expert on this subject..." No kidding, Bernice thought to herself. "...but the regression analysis portends a recalibration of the fingular taps on the torsion bar systems that requires periodic confluescence." Even his English was unintelligible.

About an hour into the meeting, Willard announced, "Let's just take a quick break. I'll begin again in about five minutes." To Willard, about five minutes generally meant fifteen.

Two and a half hours after it started, Bernice wondered if the meeting would ever end. "There's just one more topic I'd like to cover, so I'll be brief," Willard said. Bernice counted four more topics during the eight-minute soliloquy that followed.

When Willard said, "So finally in conclusion..." two members were actually asleep. He eventually finished. "Well, thank you everyone. That was a very good meeting." Compared to being eaten alive by alligators, that is, Bernice reflected. Maybe next time she would find herself conveniently absent by catching a communicable disease prior to one of Willard's meetings: Fake-Itis Horibilis.

Don't attend meetings that don't have a goal,
And only show up if you have a key role.

CHAIR A MEETING

A good sign that either the meeting or some of the people are superfluous is when they try to get out of coming. ROBERT HELLER

The role of a chairperson at a formal meeting is to guide the meeting and to act as a neutral arbiter to the conduct of members. In a less formal meeting, the chairperson may take a more active and less neutral role. The challenge is to find a balance between a high level of involvement, where the chairperson dominates, and a laissez-fair approach, where the meeting runs out of control. Regardless of the kind of meeting, the chairperson must be authoritative and firm. This means taking responsibility for sticking to the agenda, watching the time, allowing everyone to speak and moving items through as expeditiously as possible.

Starting the Meeting Effectively

Before the meeting starts, arrange seating so everyone can see one another clearly. Post the agenda on a flip chart or white board, if you haven't already distributed typed copies. Practice with your audiovisual aids beforehand to ensure that overheads can be seen easily or that other visual aids work as they should.

The first and most obvious way to control a meeting is to

start on time. You've probably heard the phrase "we'll just wait a few minutes for everyone to arrive" too many times by now. Delaying the meeting ends up punishing those who arrive on time and rewarding those who are late. It also sets a pattern. Once people know that meetings never start on time, they never show up on time.

So you've decided to start on time, but it's clear that not everyone has arrived. In that case, do something, do anything to create a sense of direction so that when people walk in late, they know they are late. Here are some possible "opening gambits," to borrow a chess term:

- Make a few minor announcements.
- Conduct an ice-breaker exercise.
- Ask people to fill out a survey (perhaps on late meetings).
- Ask for minor reports to be delivered.

Review What Will Happen

When most attendees are present, review the agenda and ask if anyone has anything else to add. If you haven't previously established a protocol, review meeting procedures. For instance, how long will people be allowed to speak? Will you aim for consensus through a show of hands, or will you institute more formal parliamentary procedure? In general, voting is not a good idea, since it creates a win-lose situation, rather than a win-win situation.

When latecomers arrive, don't review everything that has taken place for them. At the end of the meeting, ask the members if they would like to start on time at the following meeting. Get their concurrence to do so and follow through. Ask if the group would like to levy a fine for latecomers—one dollar for a local charity perhaps.

Get to Know Everyone

At the beginning of the meeting, introduce members or have

them introduce one another. For a novel way of handling introductions, ask participants to tell who they are, what they do and why they are at the meeting. You can also ask them to mention one thing that most people don't know about them. But add a catch. In the first sentence, tell them they may not use their names or the words "I," "me," "my" or "mine." Also, they may not repeat a first sentence used by another member. This is a good ice breaker and an original way to create familiarity within the group.

Even though everyone will have been introduced, they might forget who is who. To prevent this, place cards in front of people with their names so they know how to address one another. This practice helps you as chairperson also, if you don't know everyone's name. If cards aren't available, fold an 8 1/2-by-11-inch sheet in thirds, write a name on one of the panels, and prop the sheet up, tent style, on the table.

Take Control of the Meeting

Another key role for the chairperson is to ensure that people stick to the agenda. You should interrupt when the discussion meanders and bring it back on track. The more blunt, the better. Also, cut short members who repeat themselves. Some people take a long time to make a point. Discourage these major talkers from taking up too much time. "Manuella, I can see you've got some good points, but I want to make sure we hear some other points of view…"

As chairperson, avoid stating your own position unless absolutely necessary. Act as mediator, facilitator and coach, rather than as dictator, and aim to achieve group consensus.

The chairperson is responsible for seeking out dissenting points of view. Try to draw out the quiet people in the corners. Ask them straight out if they have anything they'd like to add. Be aware of body language, particularly when people react squeamishly. You can simply say, for example, "Dimitri, you don't seem too happy about that…" and wait for them to speak. Clarify major points along the way, rather than allowing confusion to set in later on. Then, state agreements when they've been reached.

If you face a situation where everyone wants to speak at once, ask people to raise their hands if they want to make a point. Write down their names on a sheet in front of you and allow them to speak in turn. As they make their points, cross their name off your list.

Finishing Well

Aim for a specific finishing time and let people know when it is approaching. Discussions tend to speed up as deadlines become imminent. After the meeting, you or your delegate should confirm agreements in writing.

Ask people to prepare for the next meeting by formulating their recommendations prior to arriving. Meetings run more smoothly when people do their "homework" in advance.

Keep long meetings under two hours. Generally, meetings go on for a long time because participants have done too little work beforehand and are unprepared. By recording and keeping track of the time you spend at meetings, you'll soon find that they will become more efficient. Exceptions to meeting length can be made for all-day strategy meetings, brainstorming sessions or training.

TIME TRIVIA

Executives have poor opinions of meetings. The following table shows the percentage of executives who are "bothered a lot" by various meeting dynamics.

Factor	% bothered a lot
People drifting off subject	83%
Participants' lack of preparation	77%
Questionable effectiveness	74%
People not listening	67%
People's wordiness	62%
Length of time taken	60%
People not participating	51%
Emotional outbursts	41%

PAUL RICE, TIMESOURCE

When the result of a meeting is to schedule more meetings, it usually signals trouble. KEVIN MURPHY

In order to speak short on any subject, think long. HUGH HENRY BRACKENRIDGE

That's a Great Idea,
but There's Always a But

One morning, at a small desk, in a small office, somewhere in a small corner of the slightly more immense Waffle's Widgets Division, Lloyd Longstocking pondered a problem. He needed to generate some innovative publicity ideas for the company's new Suit Yourselves Dance Club. The club was a novel, even bizarre concept. It allowed patrons to select their own music on individual headsets. That way everyone could dance to their own favorite tunes.

Lloyd decided to assemble a team of the brightest minds to assist him. Unfortunately, most of them were dead. So, instead, he scheduled a meeting of twelve senior managers for a Tuesday morning at nine o'clock in the board room.

At the appointed time, Lloyd arrived, only to discover the room was empty. He waited. The room continued to be empty. Forty-five minutes later, Lloyd was still there. The room, not surprisingly, was still empty, though none the less perturbed for it. Lloyd later learned that owing to a slight mix up on the confirmation letter, the managers had erroneously convened in a small motel room outside the city to discuss streamlined systems for eliminating cracked fingernails.

Lloyd called a second meeting a week later, where, as chairperson, he introduced the topic. "Gentlemen…" he began.

"And ladies," a voice chipped in.

"Gentlemen and ladies," Lloyd corrected, "I've gathered…"

"Uh, excuse me," a voice interrupted from the rear of the room. "Since you've accommodated both sexes, would you mind terribly referring to those of us who are doctors as doctors?"

"Yes, well, ladies and gentlemen, and doctors, I wanted to…"

"Pardon me," another voice interrupted, "but while you're at it, I'm a member of a local community group, and, well, it certainly would be nice if I was referred to as Lord High Potentate."

Lloyd was becoming visibly perturbed. His veins bulged. His sweat poured. His left foot flew up on to the table. "Folks," he announced as he delicately replaced his foot on the floor, "I want to get some ideas from you on how to create some publicity for Suit Yourselves."

"What?" cried a voice from the back. "I thought this was a meeting of the Mouse Pad Procurement Advisory Committee."

"I'm afraid not," said Lloyd.

"Oh well, in that case I'll stay anyway," said the voice in a rather offhand and illogical concession to whatever it was that it was conceding to.

Lloyd turned to the flip chart. To facilitate note taking, he had arranged for a number of visual aids to be set up by the office services department. Unfortunately, the white board was unavailable. It had got into a fight with a delinquent blackboard and was slightly damaged. Flip charts were the preferred alternative, though there was no tape to stick the sheets to the walls. Chewing-gum would have to do. Lloyd wrote on the chart: "ideas for getting publicity." He explained the Suit Yourselves concept and addressed the group, "Okay, let's begin. Any ideas?"

The response was silence. Utter quiet. Really, really quiet. A tiny flea, perched on the end of a pin lying on the floor, dropped an even tinier pin. Heads turned as it broke the silence.

"Hmm, okay, can anyone think of anything at all?" pleaded Lloyd.

More silence.

More and more and more silence.

Then finally, and with some hesitation, "A dance contest?" a sales manager asked.

"No," piped in Desmond Gargarella, a product manager. "Last time we tried that, we got a panel to judge the entries and we almost got in trouble for encouraging lascivious behavior. Or wait, maybe it was jay walking. I can't remember."

"Perhaps you should publicize the best beer prices in town," countered one of the senior managers.

"No. You see, the problem is that we need an advertising campaign, not publicity," said an account executive who had been invited from the advertising agency.

"Yeah, well, that last commercial you guys showed was the pits!" the operations manager barked.

"Well, if the budget hadn't been cut back at the last minute..." the account executive answered.

"Why don't we just promote it through word of mouth?" asked another voice.

"Sure, you've got a big one..."

"Look, why don't we give it a new name? I never liked Suit Yourselves much."

"So, you have a better idea?"

"Uh, no."

"I don't like this publicity thing at all."

"Is lunch being served?"

After much tiresome bickering, Lloyd was left with two ideas. Neither could be implemented without tripling the budget or procuring an atomic warhead. And that was the easy part.

Forced to adjourn the meeting, he asked the group to reconvene in two weeks to consider some further ideas. Perhaps the next time the process would flow like a steady stream, instead of like sluggish molasses. Despite grumbling about having better things to do, the attendees agreed to go ahead with another session. Lloyd agreed in return to provide free lunches and tickets to a local octogenarian mud-wrestling match. It's been said that ideas are a dime a dozen. For Lloyd, it was more like six hundred dollars a pair.

To create new ideas let your mind start to play,
Suspend all your judgments 'til some other day.

BRAINSTORM EFFECTIVELY

A crank is a man with an idea
until it succeeds. Mark Twain

Brainstorming is a method of generating a large number of original ideas or creative solutions to problems. It works because of synergy. When a number of people brainstorm together, their collective creativity results in ideas that no one person might have thought up. Productive brainstorming confirms the old adage that the whole is greater than the sum of the parts.

Gather Your Team

Gather a team of three to seven people in a quiet place away from distractions. Groups larger than this tend to become cumbersome. Backgrounds should be diverse, so don't limit yourself to the people on your own team. Bring along experts, but also invite people who may not have a connection with the issue being considered. Their objectivity and distance from the issues will provide a fresh perspective.

You might try a warm-up exercise, using the principles of brainstorming outlined below. For instance, list as many uses for a brick as possible, or create a solution to global warming. These activities will warm up people's minds and will give you a chance to clarify the guidelines in case someone isn't following them properly.

Outline the Rules of Brainstorming

When you're ready to start in earnest, clearly state the issue to be discussed and the desired outcome. For instance, "People seem to think our product is old-fashioned, so the objective is to come up with ideas for a new radio advertising campaign." Give the group any relevant background information.

Then it's time to go into full gear. Appoint someone to transcribe the ideas on a flip chart, and start asking for ideas. Use the four rules of brainstorming:

- Quantity is desired, not quality. People should try to submit as many ideas as possible in rapid succession.
- Postpone evaluative comments until later. Ask people to avoid phrases such as:
    - We tried that already.
    - We had that idea already.
    - I'm not sure about that.
    - The boss won't allow that idea.
    - That will be too expensive.
    - I'm not sure if this is too wacky, but...
    - There's not enough time, staff or resources for that.
    - That's not going to work.
    - I don't like it.
    - It's too expensive.
- Build on others' ideas by "hitchhiking." When someone suggests something, add onto their idea or find another new idea that connects with it in some way.
- The more outrageous the ideas the better. Just keep coming up with them and allow your imagination to go wild.

Watch out for occasional violations of the second rule. Even phrases such as "we've listed that already" are a form of judgment and should be avoided.

Determine how much time the group will spend discussing each item, and be aware of the passage of time. Try to control the order of speakers so that only one person speaks at a time. But if things get slightly unruly, let the energy flow and build. The person transcribing will have difficulty keeping up, but that's to be expected. Write the ideas on a flip chart for everyone to see. A flip chart also allows you to type and circulate the ideas after the meeting.

You can schedule a good part of a day for a brainstorming meeting. The actual idea-generating sessions can be completed in a half hour. However, as you consider variations on the problem or as you look at other problems, you can capitalize on the group synergy and conduct a series of mini-sessions. So allocate enough time for the sessions. Include time for training and a warm-up exercise beforehand and for evaluating ideas at the end.

TIME TRIVIA

When sales reps use the telephone, the average length of a call to a customer is 9 minutes. The average length of a call to a new prospect is only 5 minutes.
PACE PRODUCTIVITY RESEARCH

MASTERING TECHNOLOGY

Imagine if every Thursday your shoes exploded if you tied them the usual way. This happens to us all the time with computers, and nobody thinks of complaining. JEFF RASKIN

Voice Mail Jail

"Thank you for calling. You have reached 416-762-3453, in case you've already forgotten what number you dialed. This is Dudley A. Nili of First Systems Group International Global Limited, Fish Hooks and Knitting Needles Division.

It's Tuesday May the first, at eight a.m., eastern standard time. I'm either on the phone, or not at my desk, or involved in an interminably long meeting with a rather simple minded accountant whose idea of timeliness involves cooking a three-minute egg for five minutes.

"If you require immediate assistance, please press zero, although the likelihood of your inquiry being handled in any reasonable length of time is about the same as the chances of a snowstorm in the Sahara, in which case you may wish to call back and go through all this rigmarole again.

"Or you can stay on the line and leave a message after the long, continuous beep immediately following the series of short, intermittent beeps. State your name, phone number, time of calling, astrological sign and reason for calling.

"Please leave a detailed confidential message as no one else has access to my voice mail, with the possible exception of my assistant, who occasionally pokes around looking for juicy tidbits. Oh, and my boss too. And the office manager, come to think of it. After you leave a message, you may press '1' if you wish to hear this message again, press '2' if you wish the directory for someone else or press '3' to listen to an irritatingly loud, high-pitched screech.

"Instead of leaving a message, if perhaps you would like, you may wish to page me at 416-410-7792, if you want. When an obnoxious bully answers, simply ask for pager number B6215493512CX and leave a brief message not exceeding 35 characters in length, excluding your phone number, which may be up to an additional 15 characters. Don't even think about using a q or a z.

"You may also wish to call me in my car. My cellular number is 416-347-6593. If I'm not there, you may leave a message there, which I will pick up here, as soon as I get here. If you don't reach me, please be patient. There's a good chance I'm trying to track down all the messages people have been leaving me.

"Or of course you may fax me at 416-762-3301. No junk mail please, unless it's an invitation to a matchbook cover collectors' convention.

"If you wish to avoid all this, you may want to send me a letter. If you're sending it by courier, make sure the courier arrives between 10 and 11:30 a.m. or between 2 and 4 p.m. during the week, or after 4 p.m. on weekends, unless it is the last week of the month, in which case the courier should arrive before 11 a.m. on Monday, Wednesday and Friday and after 3 p.m. on all other days. My address is 4434 West 56th, East Tower, 14th Floor, Suite 12B West, North Hatley, South Dakota, USA, 46327, Earth.

"I will return your call as soon as I can, barring the remote possibility of a major thermonuclear war, or my cat getting the runs. Thank you for calling and I hope you have a nice day, particularly if you've made it all the way through this message. I'll certainly look forward to hearing from you. I'm also amenable to a Vulcan mind meld. Talk to you later. Goodbye. Wait for the beep. Gotta go. Be seeing you. Bye."

When leaving a message be clear and concise,
Don't ramble on and try to be nice.

USE VOICE MAIL EFFECTIVELY

---

*The real danger is not that computers will begin
to think like men, but that men will begin to
think like computers.* SYDNEY J. HARRIS

Voice mail was originally heralded as a great productivity tool.
And, in most cases, it is. But because of its popularity, many
people now find it a challenge to get through to "a real person."
Imagine, for instance, if everyone left their phones permanently
on voice mail. Would anything get done? Spending up to an
hour per day on voice and E-mail combined is not unusual. So,
there are a few common-sense guidelines about how to use voice
mail effectively.

Recording Your Own Voice Mail Message

Keep your voice mail greeting brief. Call your own number to
see what it sounds like to a typical user. You might discover that
your voice mail sounds faint or rushed, or that your prompts are
awkward to follow.

You may change your message occasionally for variety, but
you need not change it every day. After all, how does changing it
help those who are calling? If you're tied up in meetings all day,
but are going to be checking your mail, do you really need to
tell people this? The only time you absolutely need a date stamp

is when you'll be away for an extended period, such as a vacation when you are not taking messages. (Let's hope you're not. Otherwise, what's the point of a vacation?)

Most people are now familiar with answering machines and voice mail. So try to avoid clichés such as, "Hi, I'm not in right now, so after the beep, leave your name, your number and a brief message and I'll call you back as soon as I can." People know the routine already. Try to be a bit more creative. Use humor. Everyone loves to smile.

Ensure your automated telephone system has an easy way for people to reach a live voice. They should be able to press zero, for instance. Again, test the system by calling yourself.

Don't leave more than one number where people can reach you. Additional numbers create more aggravation for callers, especially if you have recorded messages for each phone.

If you have a car phone, use it primarily for outgoing calls. Limit the list of people who can call you there, since most of the time you are not in your car anyway. Return messages within twenty-four hours. Not all strangers are trying to sell you something; they may want to buy something.

Avoid the temptation to tell white lies on your voice mail. ("I'm in a meeting right now.") You might get caught.

Leaving Messages for Others

Plan your message before you call, especially if there is more than one item. You don't want to get caught having to look up information in the middle of a message. Be specific about why you are calling. Give a reason for your call, rather than saying, "Could you call me back?" And use the person's name. Everyone loves to hear his or her own name.

Spell your name if it is uncommon. Remember that someone is trying to type or write down your information at the other end, and this person doesn't know your name as well as you do.

When you give your phone number and name, speak very slowly. Some people give their numbers twice, but you need not do so if you say it clearly the first time.

Finally, leave a suggested time range for when you can be reached. There's no need to stay in voice mail jail forever playing telephone tag. (What a mixture of metaphors!)

TIME TRIVIA

Seven out of ten people interviewed in a survey of Fortune 1000 companies said they are overwhelmed in their professional and personal lives, sending and receiving an average of 178 messages each day by more than a dozen different means, including phone, pager, fax and Post-It note. The study said that people are inundated with so many communication tools—fax, electronic mail, regular mail, inter-office mail, voice mail, teleconferencing —that they don't know which to turn to for even the simplest tasks. As a result, more tools are sending out more messages.

GLOBE AND MAIL, REPORT ON BUSINESS

Cordless Interruptus

While making love, Frederick Titcombe's pager, cellular phone, portable fax and answering machine all rang simultaneously. Frederick had never imagined such an unlikely coincidence would occur at such an inopportune moment. Even at home, he could be tracked down! The timing could not have been worse, with the possible exception of his being interrupted while polishing his collection of souvenir Niagara Falls barometers.

In the midst of what was rapidly becoming a decreasingly passionate embrace, Frederick realized he had a difficult dilemma: Should he take the calls or continue his amorous escapade? Fortunately, as his wife Beatrice reminded him in no uncertain terms, the calls could wait.

The next day Frederick was again made aware of the often detrimental effect telephone technology was having on his life. He was returning a voice mail message from a product manager at a supplier.

"Is Desmond Gargarella there, please?" Frederick asked the product manager's assistant.

"I'll see. Would you like to hold?" was the response. Would I like to hold, Frederick wondered. Sure, about as much as he liked swallowing razor blades. Frederick listened to the hold message, a recording of "You're Having My Baby," played on an off-key xylophone and accompanied by what sounded like an alley cat in heat. The voice came back on the line, promising, "Just a minute." Four minutes passed, this time with "Purple Haze" on the xylophone. Then, "May I tell him who's calling?"

Frederick decided to take a dare. "No, let's make it a big surprise!" The assistant was not amused. As it turned out, the product manager would have to touch base with Frederick the next day. Where were all these bases that people kept touching, Frederick often wondered.

The straw that broke the Mongolian gazelle's back occurred later, when Frederick was writing a new sales strategy. He was interrupted by a phone call. He answered, and while he was on the phone, his boss walked in, interrupting his interruption. Then the intercom buzzed. It was his assistant, interrupting his boss's interruption of his caller's interruption. The fabric of the universe began to split at the seams when Frederick's secretary poked his head through the doorway. "Mind if I interrupt?" the secretary asked, interrupting the interruption of the interruption of the interruption. Frederick wondered what else could go wrong, when the fire alarm went off. Saved by the bell.

Frederick needed help. He phoned the company's guru of gurology, Crispin Quirty. "Hi, Crispin. Have you got a second to drop by my office?" Frederick asked.

"Sure," Crispin answered.

"Thanks. It will just take a minute." Time had a way of making great leaps with Frederick.

Crispin arrived a few minutes later, wearing a baseball cap on which the company's logo was emblazoned along with the slogan, "The speed of time is one second per second."

"It seems all of my high-tech tools are causing me more grief than good, and at a considerable expense too," Frederick complained. "I spend too much time answering unimportant communications, and not enough on strategic planning, budgeting and coaching. Last week, for instance, I got three junk faxes from someone try to sell a service that prevents junk faxes from being received."

"Yes, well, for a lot of people, each new piece of technology simply adds another way for them to be out of touch with one another," Crispin answered wryly. "Try blocking your time by returning calls at the same time every day. And there should be someone available in the department to answer emergency problems. The receptionist and your voice mail can inform callers of the best time to reach you, such as between eight and nine o'clock. And relieve yourself of menial communications. Invest the time to train your staff."

"To relieve themselves?"

"Well, maybe that too. I've met some of them."

Frederick put Crispin's ideas to use and his productivity increased; he even found more time to spend with his wife. Celebrating their thirteenth anniversary cozily snuggled up in the process of continuing where this story began, Frederick whispered seductively. "This is it. No calls, no pagers, just you."

Then, the inevitable occurred. The bedroom door quietly opened and a small head poked through. "Daddy, can you help me with my homework?" Another day, another dilemma.

Keep your life simple, though you must stay in touch,
Don't become burdened by pagers and such.

BE EFFECTIVE ON THE PHONE

*I have never been able to understand why
it is that just because I am unintelligible
nobody understands me.* MILTON MAYER

Voice mail can work remarkably well when you're simply trading information back and forth. But sooner or later you'll simply have to talk to a live person. ("Oops, I wasn't expecting you to answer, I was expecting your voice mail.")

Prepare for the Call
Get ready for each call by reminding yourself of the purpose for your conversation. Make written notes of the key issues you wish to discuss.

Some phone calls create anxiety before you make them. If you're feeling tense, try a stress-relieving exercise. Tighten all your muscles and take a deep breath, holding this position for a count of five. Then exhale slowly and let your muscles relax. Say affirmations to yourself, such as, "I am confident and relaxed." Take a deep breath again, hold it, then breathe out. Breathe slowly and concentrate on feeling the tension leaving your body. Picture yourself in a calm spot, at the cottage or on the beach, and hold that thought. Visualize serenity. Remember, also, that most people you reach will probably enjoy a conversation with you if you handle the call courteously and professionally. Few people ever want to embarrass you.

Standing up when making calls adds to your authority and can relax you, as well. You might also try a telephone headset. It leaves your hands free for typing, writing and sorting papers. Some people put a mirror in front of themselves. They look at it and smile prior to making a call. This increases self-confidence.

After you reach someone on the phone, try starting with, "Good morning," or, "Good Afternoon." These greetings establish a positive tone and accustom the person on the other end to your voice. But limit social conversation to brief comments at the beginning. Have a writing pad nearby for taking down information, or type it directly onto your computer. Type quietly, as some people dislike being recorded.

Getting Agreement

If you reach someone who is screening calls, ask for his or her name. This makes the person feel important, and the name may be useful to you if you reach them again. When you are returning someone's call, tell this to the person who is doing the screening so you'll get through faster.

If the purpose of your call is to persuade someone, use a series of short questions that make it easy for the person to say yes. Start with simple ones, then move to the more complex. Once you think you've created an agreement, use the phrase, "Will that be all right?" or find one of your own that encourages a positive response and is friendly. When closing, offer easy choices, such as, "Would Friday morning or afternoon be a good time to meet?" or, "Will you be sending that payment by mail or by courier?"

Receiving Calls Effectively

Try to answer calls on the first ring when possible. Your efficiency will impress the caller. Pronounce your own name or the company name with authority when you answer. If your business is based at home, turn off your radio and television set and close your door to noisy children. Call waiting started as a great idea, but it doesn't really help anyone. It's awkward for both parties when you have to say, "Sorry, gotta go. There's a call on the other line." Use call answer or voice mail instead. These services allow you to receive messages while you're on the line.

At work, if your voice mail is not on, ask co-workers to take detailed messages, including the caller's purpose. They should say to callers, "To help her prepare when she calls you back, can I tell her what you're looking for?"

TIME TRIVIA

The average length of an outbound telemarketing call is 5.6 minutes. The average percentage of these calls that results in a sale is 31% for business to business applications and 23% for consumer applications.

PRICE WATERHOUSE STUDY

For Office Use Only, on Pain of Death

Anthony Slobodsky removed his wooden finger to pour himself a cup of coffee. He wasn't missing a finger. Anthony's hands were each fully equipped with four digits and a regular, albeit stubby-looking thumb. The wooden finger was actually a clever device Anthony had invented for filling out the twelve-part form used for processing his sales orders. His company existed in a 1970s time warp and hadn't gotten around to computerizing their forms yet. They also played disco music at company socials.

In the past, Anthony's efforts to press firmly enough to make an impression through all twelve copies had resulted in occasional misfortune. Pencils tips broke, and pens created small lacerations in the paper, but the wooden finger, with its hard tip, provided the requisite pressure.

The only drawback to Anthony's device was that it didn't leave a readable impression on the first copy. No matter, though. The second copy was always sent back by an unknown clerk, having been stamped, dated, numbered, indexed, hole punched, initialed and approved. Apparently the clerk, known only as 'the Stamper,' was a veteran employee who could recite plot details and camera angles for every Star Trek episode ever aired.

The remaining ten copies of the form were distributed throughout the company. The order department kept the third copy, the fourth went to the unit manager and the fifth went to the district manager, even though this position no longer existed. Copies six, seven and eight went to production, shipping and office services. Office services wanted a copy of every form ever produced, just in case, though they had no idea what eventuality they were worried about. The ninth copy was sent to data entry, where an extensive computer report was produced, which no one ever read. Number ten found its way to the credit department, where it was used to boost the department's recycled paper quota. No one was quite sure what happened to the eleventh copy, though some copies had been seen lining a bird cage in the front lobby. Twelve was almost entirely blacked out, except for the rep's last name. Someone once calculated that the fuel used to produce the company's order forms each year was sufficient to power a small city for a week or a dozen vibrating, electric reclining chairs for a month.

Not only was there a surplus of paper, there was also a surplus of required information. Anthony found the endless series of shaded boxes a huge time waster: client codes, territory codes, product codes, postal codes, rep codes and dress codes all had to be filled out. In quiet vengeance, he took great pleasure writing in the "DO NOT WRITE HERE" spaces, usually filling them with cryptic notes to the Stamper about which Star Trek captain was better. So far that week he had spent more time filling out forms than he had in meetings with his prospects!

Three weeks later Anthony and the other fourteen sales reps gathered at their monthly sales meeting, which started precisely on time, ten minutes late. Because each rep was spending more time than expected processing orders and handling mail, the unit manager announced that a new assistant would be working exclusively for the reps to free up more selling time. The old form would be replaced with a simpler version, and the company had already begun automating the entire process. The manager then summoned the new assistant, who had just transferred from another department. He was about sixty years old, with gray, receding hair and a bit of a paunch.

"I'm looking forward to being of assistance," he said, "but I have just one request. Anthony, if you insist on writing all that TV trivia, could you please print a little more legibly? And by the way, it was definitely episode twelve."

Data that's needed should be simple and clear,
To discard the useless, have nary a fear.

HANDLE INCOMING MAIL

There is no quicker way for two executives to get out of touch with each other than to retire to the seclusion of their office and write each other notes. ALEC MACKENZIE

Incoming mail is inevitable. With the increasing proliferation of E-mail over the last few years, office workers now have to contend with both hard copy and electronic transmissions. You need to make time for mail and dispense with it quickly.

Set Aside Time

Create a block of time outside prime hours to handle mail and other paperwork. Schedule this time in your planner and stick to it. Handle your mail and your E-mail at the same time every day, not just when it comes in. When you receive mail, do one of four things: take action on it, delegate it, delete it or file it. The file where you place your mail may be either a permanent file for storage or a follow-up file for items to be dealt with later.

Time management experts recommend that you never handle a piece of paper more than once. But it's tough to avoid the "I'll just put this here for now" habit. If you still find yourself accumulating miscellaneous papers, create a "junk file" to put them in. Go through it occasionally, perhaps once a week, and don't let it get over an inch thick.

If multiple handling of the same item is an issue, consider putting a small dot in the upper corner of a piece of paper each time you handle it. The accumulation of dots will create a heightened awareness of your procrastination.

Sorting Mail

If you have an assistant, ask him or her to sort your mail before it gets to you, rerouting or throwing out items you don't need to see. Delegate mail handling for both traditional and E-mail. For items that will reach you, ask your assistant to sort them according to urgency, to highlight important aspects and to attach relevant files or information.

Open your mail in your office, not where it is delivered. Always open it near a waste basket or recycling bin.

When responding to mail, try to limit your letters, recommendations, responses and meeting requests to one page. Limit E-mail responses to a single screen. Hand write responses on paper memos from others when you can.

Try leaving redundant sections of forms blank, to see if anyone is really using them. Ask people if every report is really necessary. Prepare them only when needed, not as a regular routine.

When you receive brochures about events, decide right away whether you want to attend and write it in your calendar. If you absolutely can't yet decide, keep the brochure in a file marked 'Upcoming' and review it occasionally. Otherwise, throw out the brochure.

TIME TRIVIA

Office workers who tracked their time on general administration and paperwork spend an average of 4.5 hours per week on these activities. They engage in administration and paperwork an average of 18 times per week for 15 minutes at a stretch.
PACE PRODUCTIVITY RESEARCH

E-Mail advocates love to push the benefits of direct communication. Managers send and receive messages on a one-to-one basis. Now that secretaries don't fix their sloppy writing, the whole world wonders how they passed English 1A. DAVID BERGER

The motivation behind these tools and technologies is people's desire to speed up the process and to make it more convenient to their schedules. Instead, more and more tools are sending out more and more messages.
BILL MACKRELL, PITNEY BOWES

I'll Never Forget What's His Name

"**J**asmine, do you know the phone number for what's his name at the whatcha-ma-call-it company out in the west end?" Jasmine Foxwell sighed in disbelief at this increasingly irritating question from her befuddled co-worker Melvin Dumbrell. She fired back a volley of her own.

"It's 911!" she shouted across the bullpen.

"Wait, that's the number for emergency help," Melvin whined.

"Just what you need," she answered with a sarcastic smile.

"Forget it, I'll just find it myself." For Melvin, this was about as realistic as saying, "No problem, I'll just build a nuclear reactor in my basement." Melvin flipped open one of his four business card binders. Each was filled to the brim with dozens of business cards, contained in pages of plastic sleeves. Flip, flip, flip went the pages as Melvin's stubby fingers fumbled through. Melvin let his fingers do the walking. His fingers soon broke into a brisk trot, then into a full-out sprint as he flicked through the pages at a frantic pace. Flip, flip, flip.

He couldn't find the number, so he went to his back-up system. From a bottom drawer, he pulled out a shoe box full of personalized pens, engraved ash trays, catchy calendars, etched erasers, printed pads and stamped stationery. Each was a valuable reference tool, as each was inscribed with a customer's name and phone number. Finally, he found the name he was looking for: Sandy Hackbusch of Dewey's Drains and Ditches. He reached Sandy on the phone.

"Hi Sandy, I think we talked a couple of months ago, did we not? We didn't? Last week? Oh, I'm sorry, I mixed you up with Sidney Hackenberger." Melvin quickly pulled out his index card file, his secondary back up system, and began desperately searching through the box until he reached Sandy's card. "OK, Sandy, I've got you here, we should..." But by then the line had gone dead.

Later, Melvin decided to send out a mailing to all his telecommunications customers. Flip, flip, flip once again, as he searched to find his key contacts. As he sorted through business cards, index cards and ash trays, he got a call from a sales rep.

"Hello, Melvin, this is Darwin Pulleyblank, we met at the High Tech show seven weeks ago. A month later you asked me to call you back today. Apparently, your budget planning starts next week. Anyway..."

"Boy you have a memory. How do you know all that stuff?" asked Melvin. "I don't suppose you remember whether we talked in the morning or afternoon, do you?" Melvin asked sarcastically.

"Three twenty-eight p.m., to be precise."

"Did you go to one of those speed memory courses or something?" Melvin asked.

"Actually my memory isn't very good at all. I can even forget someone's name before I find out what it is. My kids think it's great though. I gave one of them his weekly allowance four times in the last three days. So I rely on a contact management system. It's like a phone book, but in addition to the name, address and number, I can look up the type of company, the last time I called, the president's birthday, even his pet iguana's name. Well, maybe not quite. Anyway it's all stored on my computer."

"So you can sort people any way you like?" Melvin asked.

"That's right. I was doing some research for one of the political parties, using a database. I was able to sort through politicians' names and extract those with lower-than-average IQ scores."

"How many did you get?"

"All of them. Anyway, as you can tell, I also keep notes on all of my calls, so I know exactly what we talked about last time and when we talked. Why don't you get yourself a contact management system?"

"I guess I should," Melvin answered. "What number should I call? Hold on, I had better jot this down. Jasmine, can you bring one of those writing thingies to my cuticle?"

"A pen to your cubicle perhaps?" Jasmine came to the rescue, extracting a pen from the shoe box Melvin had left on the floor. "Here, Farquharson's English School." She gave him the pen. "Maybe you should call them."

**Put customers' names on a database list,
Plus friends and suppliers who shouldn't be missed.**

TRACK CLIENTS AND PROSPECTS

> *PROGRAM (pro'-gram) n. A magic spell cast over a computer allowing it to turn one's input into error messages. v. To engage in a pastime similar to banging one's head against a wall, but with fewer opportunities for reward.* ANONYMOUS

Who you know is as important as what you know. Your network is more vast than you realize. Start with close friends, then add relatives, business associates from past jobs, suppliers, customers, university acquaintances, volunteer associates and neighbors. By keeping track of them and staying in touch, you've got a huge resource of skills, advisors and potential customers. That's why contact management systems are designed to help you keep track of everyone you know.

Manual Systems

The old-fashioned system was handwritten, three-by-five-inch cards, containing customer data, which are filed in a box alphabetically. This system used to involve a lot of copying from business cards to index cards.

For those too lazy to transcribe the information, there's the business card file. Each card is stuffed into a plastic pocket, which is then inserted into a binder. The cards are easy to store, but tough to sort through if you need to find someone's name in a flash.

To create a follow-up system, some people use the "twelve plus thirty-one" file folder system. Business cards or notes on prospects are placed in monthly file folders for follow-up. At the beginning of a month, you separate the folders into thirty-one daily follow-up file folders, depending on the number of days in the month. So each day, you simply grab the file folder for that day and see what needs to be done. The system is logical but a bit antique.

The weakness of these older manual systems is that each allows for data access on only one dimension. You can look up names alphabetically (index cards) or based on how recent they are (business card file) or based on when you should next be reaching them (twelve plus thirty-one folders). But you can't look up names on more than one criteria. Cross-referencing is next to impossible.

Contact Management Software

That's where computerized contact management systems are an excellent software investment. Each time you receive a business card, you type its information onto your database, then throw the card into your recycling bin.

Each name is a record. Within each record are a number of fields where details can be stored. They include:
- First and last name
- Business phone
- Fax
- Address (including postal code)
- Industry type
- Date last contacted
- Date for next contact
- Business relationship (supplier, customer, networking contact, etc.)

To make your database more powerful, you can set up additional

fields to include:
- Size of company
- Number of employees
- Main products
- Title of individual
- Birthday
- Anniversary
- Buying readiness
- Date of last order
- E-mail address

The number of names you can store is limited only by the memory on your computer. When you want to delete names from your contact list, don't erase their files. Instead, send the information to a second database. You never know when you might need to refer to the people again.

Neat Uses for Contact Management

You also may use a contact management system for scheduling appointments, meetings and anniversaries. Enter these dates in the "next time to call" field. Each time you contact someone, keep notes on your conversations, which you can refer to the next time. When you're ready to do a mailing, you can create labels for a mailing list, limiting the list to new prospects, for instance. For customers, you can automatically send out service letters at regular intervals.

When you receive business cards from new contacts, qualify the leads as you get them. At trade shows, put all the business cards from people you plan to call in one pocket. Put the cards of those who will simply receive a brochure in another pocket. If you get time, jot a brief note on the back, using a shorthand technique to remind yourself what to do. If people are of no interest, bend the corner as you put the card in your pocket.

When you return to your office, enter only the "good" names on your database, and throw out the cards from a contact you do not think will be worthwhile.

Your contact management system will also help you set goals and track contacts. Each month you can generate a report of how many people you contacted. This report can help sales people track their closing ratios, service reps track their customer requests or association administrators report on the number of members who are coming up for a renewal.

Other uses for a contact manager include:
• Faxing correspondence directly
• Creating simple forms
• Updating employee records
• Maintaining competitor information
• Keeping membership lists for community organizations

You can even create a sales campaign with a contact management system. Write an initial contact letter, and merge it with the names and addresses on file. Follow it up a few weeks later with another letter, depending on what has transpired in the meantime. The first letter provides the information that was requested. The follow-up letter might offer thanks for speaking on the phone and suggest a follow-up meeting the next month.

Finally, print a list of all your names and numbers and carry it with you in case you don't have access to your computer while you're on the road.

TIME TRIVIA

Almost one in five VCR owners fails a basic test of the new information age—setting a digital clock. The number 12:00 blinks endlessly on 16% of machines.

THE WIRTHLIN GROUP, A WASHINGTON POLLING FIRM

Don't Touch That Dial, It's Probably Broken

"**S**orry, the printer's jammed. Would you mind writing out your own name tag?" The man at the desk handed Samantha Pulleyblank the label and a magic-marker pen. She scribbled her name on a label and stuck it on her jacket, on the right side, of course. That way people could easily read her name when they shook her hand. Or so she had learned at a recent seminar entitled "How to meet people and wear name tags on the right side of your suit."

Tonight she was attending a seminar on how to use the Internet. It was being sponsored by Monster Ware, Inc. A successful software vendor, its biggest success had been a computer game called Bumper Cars. The game replicated driving through downtown traffic, complete with angry taxi drivers, obnoxious truck drivers, jay-walking pedestrians and Squeegee kids. The game even came with a cup of stale coffee, a map that was impossible to fold up and a pen that always ran out of ink at the worst times.

Samantha was new to computers. She had just bought one for her home-based business, and she knew there was a lot more to learn.

Samantha took her seat beside a man eating peanuts from a

bag. He offered her some as he explained to her how the nuts had been perfectly extracted from their shells by his new invention, the "Remove-a-Nut." He began to drone on about how it worked. Samantha was overwhelmed by all of his technical details, and hoped the presentation would start soon.

Just as the seminar was about to begin, one of the organizers appeared at the front of the room. "I'm sorry, we'll just be a few minutes. We have to get the projector working. Our computer works fine, but we're trying to project it onto the screen. There's coffee while you're waiting."

Samantha thought coffee might be the perfect escape from the inventor. She proceeded to a table where an automatic coffee machine had been set up. Something was wrong, though. Boiling water was leaking onto the table and a loud hissing sound was emanating from somewhere inside the machine. Samantha decided to take a pass.

Just then the room lights dimmed, then brightened again. Then they changed color and the room took on an eerie, red hue, then an institutional green. To top it off, a strobe light began to flash. Disco dancers appeared and began gyrating to Bee Gees songs. A few moments later they disappeared, as the organizers frantically adjusted a panel of switches. Their efforts eventually returned the room to a semblance of normalcy, a shade of putrid, white, institutional bland, just slightly dimmer than before. One of the organizers then walked to the front.

"We're going to start now. We apologize for missing the sound and the special visual effects and for the fact that the Queen won't be here to cut a ribbon, but I think you'll get the idea." Samantha wondered what kind of visual effects they had in store. Something morphing?

Near the end of the seminar someone from the audience asked, "Can you show us an actual demo of the Internet?"

The organizer looked forlorn. "Well, we had hoped to but we

can't get a working phone line. But I'll draw something on the flip chart and maybe you'll get the idea." This was somewhat like trying to build a model of the Eiffel Tower using a bag of fusilli pasta and a roll of tape.

The evening ended on a bang. It was the coffee machine blowing up. Samantha commented to another attendee on the way out, "Funny, for a company that's big on technology, they sure had a lot of problems getting things going tonight."

They approached the front door, which was locked. Beside it was a button and a sign that read, "For exit after hours, press here." Samantha pressed the button and heard what sounded like a doorbell from an overhead speaker. She tried the door, which wouldn't budge. She sighed, "Looks like it could be a long evening."

Technology's swell except now and then,
Gremlins creep in and bust things again.

USE VISUAL AIDS

A speech is a solemn responsibility. The man who makes a bad thirty-minute speech to two hundred people wastes only a half hour of his own time. But he wastes one hundred hours of the audience's time - more than four days - which should be a hanging offense. JENKIN LLOYD JAMES

Visual aids can help illustrate a speech, but you should not use them as a crutch. The audience's focus should be on you, the speaker, not on a screen. The best visuals have a maximum of four or five points. Graphs, bar charts and pie charts should not be cluttered with extraneous glitz. Does the chart really need to be in three dimensions, just because it looks neat, or would two dimensions suffice? Does a color slide make a difference or can you save time with a simple black-and-white overhead?

The more complicated your presentation, the more you'll need to set up beforehand and rehearse. Arrive early, check the equipment and have a back-up plan in case something goes wrong. When the presentation starts, don't dim the lights too much. Darkness isn't always necessary, and you certainly don't want people to fall asleep.

Have copies of your presentation available, so the audience will not need to take notes. But don't give them out at the beginning because people will then flip ahead of you, spoiling the drama of your presentation. Give out copies at the end.

Here are some of the visual aids available to you.

White Board

The white board is good for working sessions when you need to make quick illustrations on the fly, and when copies aren't necessary. (There are also high-tech versions that create a copy on fax paper.) You can use a white board as well for posting meeting agendas. They'll do double duty as a handy screen for an overhead projector. The biggest challenge with white boards is when you discover the pens are a bit dry, or that they're the wrong type. Test them beforehand to ensure that they'll mark adequately and erase easily. Don't forget to locate an eraser as well. Smudging the board with your hand is messy, and using paper towels is less than ideal, though they'll do in a pinch.

Flip Chart

Flip charts are good for quickly recording information. Use them in brainstorming sessions, in group discussions and for problem solving. You create a presentation with flip charts by preparing a series of pages in advance and flipping from one to the next. They're not very permanent, though, and they can become a bit shabby after repeated use. Choose a more permanent form of presentation for multiple showings.

One advantage of flip charts is that the sheets from a working session can be removed and tacked on the wall, so you may easily refer to them later. The notes from the sheets can be transcribed for circulation to participants a couple of days after the meeting.

Overhead Projector

Overhead projectors give you the combination of a formal presentation and the flexibility of a flip chart. You can prepare overhead acetates in advance, but you can also write on them as you present them. You can also use blank ones to write down audience input on the fly. Acetates are low tech, but they are highly effective.

Always set up and focus the overhead projector beforehand. There are only two controls you need worry about. The rotary knob focuses the image by moving the lens closer to or farther from the light source, just like a camera lens. The lens system can also tilt up and down. Essentially, this changes how high up the wall the image will appear. Now that you know, you won't need to learn while in the middle of a presentation.

When you set up the machine in advance, walk to the back, sit down, imagine a bunch of heads in front of you and see how the image on the screen looks. Do this when using any kind of visual aid to avoid having to say, "Can you read this at the back?"

There's a simple rule for the placement of overheads on the projector. Face the audience with the projector between them and you. If you can read the overhead you've placed on the projector, so can they. Flipping transparencies around and upside down is very unprofessional.

There are various ways to draw the audience's attention to key points. You can walk to the screen and point to areas of focus. Or you can stand beside the projector and use a pen to point. The pen creates a large shadow on the screen which directs attention. Or you can write on the transparencies, adding color and comments. Some people add the color to highlight information before the presentation begins.

Talk to the room, not to the machine or the screen behind you. You may want to stand near the screen if you wish, but never turn your back to the audience.

Slide Projector/Computer

Use slides or a computer-generated presentation for repeated programs or for very large groups. This technique is more formal than an overhead projector, but it also takes more time to prepare. Slides are appropriate when you want to show pictures, rather than just text. In speeches, aim for three to five slides per minute. The same number is appropriate for presentations that run off a computer. But be careful that the image doesn't take too long to "build."

With either of these systems, the speaker is less involved with the screen. You wouldn't walk over and point things out, for example. The advantage to slides rather than a computer system is that slides can be more easily shown on a bigger screen. Computer graphics take a lot of equipment and special projectors to achieve the same large scale.

More elaborate shows use several projectors to create special effects. Used properly though, a single projector can be very effective and less complicated.

A cardinal rule for showing slides is to never, ever, on pain of death, put yourself in a position where you have to say, "Next slide please." Use a remote control or give someone a script with the transition points marked.

Video

Video tape is more appropriate for prerecorded talks, perhaps a year-end speech by the president being sent to a large number of locations. Video also works for presentations that will be repeated many times, such as seminars, product demonstrations or tours. It can be paused along the way to solicit comments and discussion.

For large groups, it may be easier to set up multiple monitors, rather than a large screen, with its necessary special equipment.

If you're showing a video, practice turning on the tape beforehand, aiming for an efficient beginning. Videos do all sorts of strange things after the start button is pressed, unlike cassette tapes, which start right away where you last left off. When you reach the point in your presentation where the video is to begin, turn on the tape first. Then turn on the monitor so you don't create screen "snow" or white noise. Check the sound level beforehand, bearing in mind that people absorb sound.

Note one final word about the different visual aids available, a word that will make all the difference between showing sparkling professionalism and being merely adequate.

Rehearse.

TIME TRIVIA

Among those employees who spend time preparing presentations, either for internal use or for presentations to prospects, the average amount of preparation time is 1.3 hours per week.

PACE PRODUCTIVITY RESEARCH

STAYING IN CONTROL

Frankly, I don't believe people think of their office as a workplace anymore. I think they think of it as a stationery store with Danish. You want to get your pastry, your envelopes, your supplies, your toilet paper, six cups of coffee, and you go home. JERRY SEINFELD, SEIN LANGUAGE

Tribal Quest
on the Fifth Floor

L ate on a Tuesday night, Nicholas Wigglesworth's stomach began to growl. So Nicholas growled back. It was almost midnight, and Nicholas was still at work, thinking about dinner. He had skipped lunch, and breakfast was a distant memory of reheated coffee and half of a stale eggplant-zucchini muffin. With each passing minute, the hunger pangs increased.

As Nicholas reached for what turned out to be an empty pack of gum, he wondered how long he would have to stay that night. He leaned back in his chair for a brief break, contemplating the poetry of the quiet office. It surrounded him, enveloped him, soothed him, caressed him. The hands of the clock would turn, the night would march on and the dawn would come anew. Tomorrow was just turning into today, and today turning into yesterday. Bad clichés were rampant.

Nicholas decided he wasn't such a good poet after all. He was a meeting planner and his late hours were the result of incessant demands from his manager, Ridley Wantsall. Around five o'clock Ridley had dropped by for the fifth time that day. Nicholas often nicknamed him "Mr. Do It Now 'Cause I Need It." This time was no exception, as Ridley was looking for Nicholas's proposal to the National Association of Left-Handed Door Knob

Manufacturers, a room layout for the upcoming Daughters of the Canadian Revolution convention and a competitive analysis of the new U-Sleep-It-Cent-R, formerly the Sleep Eaze Hotel. (The former name had been changed after three neon sign letters had burnt out, resulting in the somewhat unfortunate designation, the Sle aze Hotel.) All this work was in addition to the revised water cooler relocation project Nicholas had already been assigned, even though he knew little about office design.

Seven hours after the meeting, Nicholas stared at a report on his computer screen. The letters started shifting back and forth, dancing on the screen like giddy zombies. Nicholas glanced away for some relief, only to see what appeared to be five overweight giraffes performing a tap dance while feather dusting a huge pile of discarded toilet paper rolls. This wasn't the sort of thing that usually happened, at least not on Tuesdays. Nicholas concluded that either he was hallucinating from food deprivation or the creative department had gone just a bit too far. They had already tried the same thing a week ago, so Willard concluded it was food that was wanting. Yes, it had been a long day, somewhere around twenty-nine hours.

Desperate for nutrition, Nicholas sallied off on a quest for food. He anticipated the challenge of the hunt, the thrill of the conquest. His heart pumped. His skin tingled.

Nicholas grabbed a letter opener and struck a defiant pose, like some ancient warrior on the prowl. Unfortunately, his hunt for food would be rather daunting, given the generally antiseptic nature of the office tower where he worked. Perhaps a less tribal approach would be more appropriate. He put the letter opener back in his drawer and pocketed a pair of nail clippers instead.

Nicholas first visited the office next to his, where Helga Dilworth kept a large jar of cookies in the shape of a rather unmenacing Dennis the Menace. Nicholas reached into the jar, only to jam his hand inside, like a mischievous character from a slap-happy cartoon. With the jar on its side, he struggled for ten minutes to extricate his rapidly swelling wrist. Finally, it popped out, as did numerous fragments of broken cookies and assorted crumbs. He gathered them up and proceeded to the boardroom.

There, on a large tray, stale bits of sandwiches remained from a luncheon meeting. To Nicholas's dismay, someone had beaten him to all the meat, salad and tomatoes, leaving three triangular slices of soggy, over-buttered bread languishing beside two limp pickles. He added them to his booty and chose a ketchup packet to brighten up the taste. But it proved to be a Herculean challenge to open the packet, resulting in a spray of bright red stains decorating his shirt and tie. He took another packet and wisely snipped it open with his nail clippers.

He needed something to wash this banquet down with. The water cooler had temporarily disappeared, a result of Nicholas's own relocation project. The coffee machine was empty, but nearby were numerous one-ounce coffee creamers. He pried the lid off each one, pouring the contents into a stained coffee cup until he had the semblance of a drink.

Now he was ready for a gourmet meal. Unfortunately, all he had was a pickle and ketchup sandwich, followed by a cookie crumb dessert and washed down with half a cup of coffee creamer. Nicholas reflected on his late hours. These long evenings weren't exactly to his liking. He wondered if there was a better way to handle all the assignments that kept being thrown at him. But for now, life was all right. His appetite had been sated. His reports would get finished. His hunt had been a success.

You're in charge of your job, of that there's no doubt,
Manage your manager and things will work out.

MANAGE YOUR MANAGER

It is those who make the worst use of their time who most complain of its shortness.

JEAN DE LA BRUYERE

Employees expect to be managed by their managers. But just as important is the need for employees to manage upwards. This means communicating with your manager and keeping one step ahead of him or her by anticipating needs and providing information in a timely way. The result is that your boss will stay a comfortable distance, providing direction and guidance only when needed, not when you least expect it.

Meet Regularly

If you don't already meet regularly, ask your manager if you can establish weekly meetings. At these meetings you can provide updates and receive direction on major projects.

You can also learn your manager's expectations of you. If deadlines are unclear, clarify them for each request your manager makes. Ask your manager to place the projects he or she assigns in order of priority.

But even with careful planning, your boss will still occasionally interrupt you. Treat these interruptions like any other. Ask her if the two of you could book a short meeting later in the day, rather than meeting now while you're busy working on an important project. Be humble, but assertive. If you're worried about the frequency of interruptions, note each time she drops by and track either the time spent or the number of occasions. Report these statistics to your manager. She may be unaware of how often she interrupts you.

Also carefully plan your communications. Bunch your updates together. Don't go to your manager every half hour with news of phone calls or new ideas. Put them together and visit your boss once per day, except for emergencies.

Ensure There Are No Surprises

In the meantime, take responsibility instead of asking for unnecessary guidance. But always adhere to the "no surprises" principle and let your manager know what you're doing. For example, inform your manager, "This is the new ad copy. Unless I hear from you by next Tuesday, I'll send it to the printer." This statement shows that you're taking control, more than asking, "Does this copy seem OK to you?" Inevitably, changes will come back. Take time to develop this trust, though. Your manager should know what's going on, and the quality of your performance is often directly related to making your boss look good.

When your workload becomes overwhelming, you shouldn't challenge your boss, but you may need to tactfully ask questions about new and unexpected assignments. These questions will help differentiate major from minor requests:
- How will this increase customer service?
- How will this help us achieve our departmental goals?
- How will this aid in my development?
- How will this allow us to increase productivity?
- Where does this fit into the strategic goals we established?
- What decision do you expect to make with the report you've requested.

The more you know about where your manager is going, the greater the commitment you can make. Tell him or her this. Keep communication with your manager as efficient and casual as possible. Never type notes or memos, unless asked. Handwritten messages are sufficient. Or use E-mail or voice mail.

TIME TRIVIA

Most office employees don't spend much time with their managers, as it turns out. Among those who tracked their time on this activity, the average is only 78 minutes per week. This represents 4 meetings of about 19 minutes each per week.

PACE PRODUCTIVITY RESEARCH

In Search of the Elusive Parking Spot

"Excuse me, kind citizen, how does one to get to Whiffen's Wallets and Widgets?" My friend Aldous Dulmage had stopped the car to ask directions from a perplexed passerby. As it turned out, the pedestrian was slightly less helpful than the large sign that said, "Downtown This Way." I was in the passenger seat and pointed to a dusty cellular phone.

"Why don't we just call and ask for directions?" I wondered aloud.

"Fifty cents a minute, that's expensive," Aldous answered. He began wrestling with a map he was trying to unfold, while driving the car with one hand. When this became no hands, I thought better of the situation and took over as navigator. I plotted a course on the heap of map, which seemed to have a mind of its own. According to the coordinates, our destination appeared to be somewhere in the lake. And if spreading the map out in the cramped car wasn't difficult enough, folding it up later was like trying to refold a parachute in a broom closet.

When we appeared to be getting close, I pointed to a parking lot. "Let's pull in there, it's only seventy-five cents per half hour." The lot quickly became a memory as we zoomed past it, continuing our search. We eventually spotted the store, only to embark on a quick trip around the block that would eventually take twenty minutes. We advanced down alleyways, bombed down boulevards, inched through intersections and careened around corners, in a fruitless search for free parking. Aldous loathed paying for parking; to him free parking and half-price movie nights were fundamental rights. Finally Aldous spotted a parking meter, which stood like a lone sentinel guarding a precious spot for him.

"Well, it's a compromise, but it'll do. Fifty cents for an hour is a lot, though," he lamented.

I responded, "Do you realize we're a fifteen-minute walk from the store?" My comment fell on deaf ears.

As we approached our destination, Aldous developed a yearning for a Crunchy Wizzo chocolate bar. Stopping at a local variety store, he discovered a long queue of people at the counter buying seven-dollar tickets for a unique lottery that guaranteed winnings of at least five dollars. Aldous, in his ever-mindful-of-every-cent manner, pronounced that this was not a wise investment, while he waited five minutes to get ten cents change from a dollar.

"Aldous, why not just leave the dollar and let them keep the change? You'd only be out ten cents," I pleaded.

"Oh, no, couldn't do that," he said as we passed the time watching some fresh paint dry. We finally got to Whiffen's. Aldous bought a wallet on special, saving himself an enormous $1.28 in the process. Was he proud!

"Aldous, do you realize this whole trip, including driving, looking for a spot and walking took over an hour? All for a measly savings of $1.28. How much do you make an hour, anyway?" Aldous answered that, unlike lawyers, he didn't bill for his hours. As a sales rep, he was paid on commission.

"Suppose you put a value on your time," I continued. "You earn about $70,000 a year; that's $1,300 a week, or $8 for every hour of the week! But you just spent a lot of time to save $1.28. Consider your opportunity cost. An hour per day is about $3,000 per year!"

"Yes I suppose, oh mighty calculator brain. But that's getting a bit obsessive isn't it?"

"Well, you're the guy who's always trying to earn more money. You have to think about how you spend your time, not just how you spend your money."

"You really do go on about this time stuff," he muttered.

"It's not about time—it's about results," I answered. "What's more important to you; driving around in frustration looking for free parking or spending a quiet afternoon with your family? How you invest your time makes a difference."

Aldous looked pensive. Finally something was sinking in. It was the front tire of his car that had slipped into a pot hole.

Two weeks later Aldous told me the good news about how he was putting a greater value on his time as a result of our discussion. He was beginning to spend much more time with his son. "Just one problem," he said. "I told him about the value of time and he really took it to heart. The smart alec figures I've doubled the time I play with him, so now he wants his allowance doubled. Help!"

Your time is worth money so don't waste it all,
Don't get too worried about matters too small.

PLAN FOR BUSINESS TRAVEL

*Natives who beat drums to drive off evil spirits
are objects of scorn to smart Americans who
blow horns to break up traffic jams.*

MARY ELLEN KELLY

So you have to travel. But is your trip really necessary? Consider doing your business be done by phone, fax, letter, E-mail or video conference instead. Or, following the principles of delegation outlined in an earlier chapter, send someone else in your place.

Local Travel

If you definitely need to meet, driving around town can take a major chunk out of your day. On occasion, ask the other person to come to you. Tell him that you have all of the information handy at your fingertips at your office, so it would be better to meet there. If you really must travel, combine the meeting with trips to different contacts in the same area.

Plan for extra travel time during rush hours, or avoid scheduling meetings during these hours altogether. Meetings that start between 8:00 and 9:30 a.m. and between 4:30 and 6:00 p.m. will require greater traveling time.

Don't waste time circling the block looking for free parking or an inexpensive meter. A small investment in a parking lot will save valuable minutes. Assume that your time is worth at least $1 per minute.

Take the unconventional route. Sometimes crosstown, one-way streets are faster than packed expressways.

Overnight Trips

Delegate all of the planning to an assistant or a travel agent. You could make your own travel plans or check out departure times on the Internet, but this isn't what you're paid to do. There is a better use of your time.

On long trips, ask a neighbor, friend or relative to keep an eye on your property, look after your house, pets and plants and pick up your mail and newspaper. Leave a phone number where you can be contacted. Use timer switches on lights at home to make the house look occupied.

Checklist For Packing

When packing, make up a standard checklist of items to take along.

Personal Care and Medical

- allergy medicine
- insect repellent
- antiseptic
- pain relief tablets
- antacid
- bandages
- stomach remedy
- car sickness products
- soap/shampoo
- toothbrush/toothpaste
- razor
- cosmetics
- contact lens accessories
- alarm clock

Clothing
- suit/dress
- socks/stockings
- shirts/blouses
- underwear
- tie/accessories
- casual shoes
- running shoes
- fitness outfit
- swimsuit
- sunglasses
- travel iron

Business Items
- briefcase
- pens
- note pad
- sales materials
- agenda
- dictation recorder
- telephone list
- calculator
- laptop computer
- money
- time planner
- business cards

Money and Documents
- wallet/purse
- passport
- driver's license
- tickets

Handy Packing Tips

- Fill shoes with rolled socks and small underwear and other easily misplaced items such as rolled ties and scarves. This is a good way to fill hollows in the luggage. Wear your largest shoes to save space.
- Pack a small, plastic trash bag to place your soiled clothing in before returning it to the luggage.
- Some items should be placed in your carry-on bag, not in checked luggage. These items include passports and visas, tickets, travel documents, traveler's checks, credit cards, cash, cameras, jewelry and identification. It might also be useful to carry maps, guidebooks, and pocket dictionaries with you.
- Ensure you have the correct inoculations.
- Make sure passports and visas are up to date.
- Don't take too much cash with you; traveler's checks are safer.
- For short trips by air, take only carry-on luggage to save waiting time. Ship heavy items in advance to save strenuous lifting en route.
- Make sure assignments are clear for subordinates during your absence.

TIME TRIVIA

For those who travel as part of their work, travel takes up 4.5 hours per week. That's the equivalent of 18 trips of 15 minutes each, or about 10% of their work time. This doesn't count the time also spent getting to and from work.

PACE PRODUCTIVITY RESEARCH

Backpack Sacks

Backpack sacks with hanging straps,
Well-worn guides and crumpled maps.

Dusty buses plow their way,
On roughened roads that have no say.

Bare-lit rooms with musty air,
Yellowed walls and floors laid bare.

> So this is travel!
> Well I'm impressed,
> Come on dear,
> We must get dressed.

Dribbling sinks that try their best,
Candles on a broken chest.

Foreign talk a garbled tongue,
Spoken out by old and young.

Ancient ruins out of tune,
Cathedral spans might fall down soon.

So this is travel!
It's nice to roam,
Let's have a burger,
Like back at home.

Tattered jeans with broken seams,
Faded out like worn-out beams.

Tasteless discos crowd the shore,
Music blaring, blast some more.

Snotty kids with dirty feet,
Crumpled shirts, a smelly sheet.

So this is travel!
It seems so nice,
The beer is warm,
Let's get some ice.

Bare-lit bulbs for bedroom light,
Ugly bugs crawl 'round at night.

Sitting crowds on stuffed full crates,
Eating from their plastic plates.

Winding lines of grumbling hordes,
Holding tight on luggage cords.

So this is travel!
There's quite a lot,
Just stand right there,
I'll get this shot.

MAKE THE BEST
OF YOUR TRAVELING TIME

A tourist is a fellow who drives thousands of miles so he can be photographed standing in front of his car. EMILE GANST

Better planning leads to better trips. There are also some strategies you can employ when you're en route to save time and to get more out of your trip.

Take a taxi or a limousine to the airport to save on parking time and to allow you to work en route. When traveling by car, listen to instructional tapes or CDs. Create your own cassette tape club by pooling tapes with others. Listen to the radio for news and public affairs to cut down on time spent reading the paper or watching the news on television.

If you want to work on a plane or train, don't sit next to a business associate, unless you need to confer. Always take extra work and reading materials for unexpected travel delays. Keep a spare set of brochures, order forms or samples in your car in case you forget to bring them along. Bring, as well, a charger or spare batteries for your laptop.

When You're There

- Make sure the water is drinkable and avoid ice in drinks and food that hasn't been washed, such as salad.

- Obtain the proper power adapters for all of your electronic equipment. Include electric razors and blowdryers.
- Use the hotel safety deposit box for valuables, and don't leave valuables on the beach or in a car.
- Always advise the police of any loss or theft and make sure you obtain a police report.
- If traveling to a foreign country, have some currency exchanged in advance to save on exchange rates.
- Take a narrated bus tour when you first arrive in a new city. This tour gives you a chance to get an overview of the city and to determine which places you want to spend time visiting.
- Change your money in a bank, never on the street to avoid rip-offs and fake money.
- Keep important papers, such as passports, some cash, and tickets, in a traveler's pouch or vest for quick access.
- Be prepared to demonstrate the operation of your electronic equipment at airport security. Check that your batteries are working.
- Dress in layers. Wearing a windbreaker over a sweater, shirt, blouse and T-shirt allows more versatility than does only one light layer and one heavy layer.
- Keep notes in a journal on what you do on a trip. When you get back home, place them in a 'Trip Notes File.' Label each file with the place and date, including brochures, etc. The notes are helpful if you want to go back to a hotel or a restaurant you liked.
- Check and keep in mind the emergency exits and procedures at your hotel when arriving.
- Ask for a cash price when settling a bill or getting a quote. Small operators have to incur excessive credit card service charges, bank deposit charges and bank withdrawal charges, to say nothing of the paperwork and the possibility of bogus

cards or checks. Many operators will extend an automatic discount of 5 percent or more.

- Never answer your hotel room door without verifying who the person is. Call the front desk and ask if a member of the hotel staff is supposed to have access to your room and for what purpose.
- Before leaving on a trip, check the Internet for accommodations. The Internet often provides sight-seeing information, weather conditions and pictures of destinations.
- Photocopy the pages of travel books relevant to the area you are visiting rather than taking entire books, to cut down on weight.

Handling Matters Back at the Office

For long business trips, ask a secretary or an assistant to summarize key points from your mail and to send or fax them to you. Phone the office at a set time every day, so others will know they can reach you if urgent matters arise. But resist the urge to retrieve your voice mail too frequently. Most people will be happy if you get back to them within twenty-four hours. Schedule the next meeting before you leave the last one. Deal immediately with notes, expense accounts and follow-up activities when you get back.

TIME TRIVIA

Japanese are entitled to seventeen and a half paid vacation days, but they don't tend to take them. In some companies, managers are so insistent that employees make use of this break that they bribe them with money. In addition, most firms have shortened the work week from a rigorous six days to five and a half.

In India, employees are legally entitled to one month off per year. If they would rather work, however, they get a cash bonus.

Workers in France and Italy take off about a month in the summer, traditionally in August.

The vacation requirement in Sweden is twenty-five days. Three consecutive weeks are legally guaranteed in summer, and the rest are provided as needed. At least half of Swedish businesses close for the month of July. Swedes can even bank a week a year and take ten paid weeks after five years.

West Germans have between six and seven weeks per year in time off—one month in summer and two weeks in winter. It's the law. Also included is an extra month's bonus pay.

Topping the list is the Netherlands. It offers the most paid vacation days—up to thirty-six for workers with seniority.

The average U.S. worker gets only fourteen paid vacation days.

(REPORTED IN PSYCHOLOGY TODAY JULY/AUGUST 1989 FROM STATISTICS GATHERED BY 'CBS THIS MORNING')

If You're Losing Your Mind, Check the Sofa Cushions

D r. Ida Denter poked a small probing device into Melvin Dumbrell's mouth and asked, "I didn't leave my car keys in there did I?" Melvin mumbled a muffled "mmff mmff." This was the same response he gave for a series of equally awkward questions.

"Do you think it will rain this weekend?"

"Mmff, mmff."

"Taxes are pretty high, aren't they?"

"Mmff, mmff."

"Did I hear somewhere that your boss is embezzling money from your company?"

"Mmff. Mmff!!" This time Melvin sounded indignant. So it was true. His boss was embezzling money. Either that, or he was reacting to the sight of an object in Dr. Denter's hand that was now hovering ominously above his mouth. Suffice to say, it was not a lollipop.

Dr. Denter was proficient in pulling, capping, filling, filing and drilling teeth. She also fixed them. Pain was her friend, plaque her enemy. She was the epitome of Ambrose Bierce's definition of a dentist; a prestidigitator who, putting metal into your mouth, pulls coins out of your pocket.

But despite her considerable dental skills, she could never seem to remember where she put her car keys. She had looked everywhere else throughout her clinic, so why not Melvin's mouth? Although she didn't find them there, she did pull out a stringy bit of corn, a couple of raspberry seeds and a rather gnarled, yet intact, plastic cap from a cheap pen. Melvin was her last patient of the day. After he left, Ida contemplated how she would get home.

She entered her office for one last search through the wave of clutter that was a constant reminder of her inability to throw anything out. A set of golf clubs were propped up next to a filing cabinet, which was crammed with files. Beside it was a desk, its drawers bursting with literature from suppliers. Near the window, a bookshelf, was stuffed with books two rows deep. On top of it, more books and magazines were piled three feet high. Ida worried that the whole thing might career over someday, if it didn't collapse under its own weight first. A second desk was covered with billing forms and correspondence. There were also casts of teeth and models of jaws stacked on top of some abstract art. Ida wasn't quite sure anymore which was which. Next to them was a promotional doll from a toothpaste manufacturer—Tooty the Toothie. When a lever was pulled on the back, its teeth turned from a gleaming white to a dingy yellow, and several teeth disappeared. Kids loved it. Ida frantically searched over and under everything looking for her keys.

Thirty minutes later, she resigned herself to taking a taxi home. Just before she left, she heard the office answering machine sputter into life. Ring. Click. Bfrzzzzalop. Click. "Hellooooo," said the machine in slow motion. "You've reached the office of Doctorrrrr Dennnterrrr. We fix teeth. Pleeeease leave a messssssage."

"Hi Ida, it's Sandford. Did you remember our dinner date for tonight? I guess you're on your way home, so I'll try there. Look forward to seeing you. Hugs and kisses my sweetums. Yum yum

yum." Ida thought Sandford was a doll, but sometimes his saccharine sweetness was a bit much.

As she waited for the taxi, Ida looked again through her purse for her car keys, as if they might have magically appeared within the last half hour. Things had become a bit messed up in there; a half-eaten, half-melted chocolate bar was stuck to tickets for the opera from three weeks ago, which she had never used. Oh well, it had received bad reviews anyway. A mangled pack of gum, receipts for groceries, three hair brushes, broken lipstick containers, multiple date books, pens that didn't work, mirrors, eyeshadow, and another tooth model were all jumbled together.

When Ida got home, she let herself in, using a spare key that she kept hidden in a pot on her porch. Rushing to the hall table, she checked the bowl where she normally left her spare keys. There were thirty-eight keys buried in the bowl, which was also stuffed with old junk mail, thousands of pennies, more pens that didn't work, receipts, paper clips, hand tools, a corkscrew and a partridge in a pear tree. Ida had no idea what most of her spare keys were for, but she hung on to them anyway, as if some day she would go on a door-opening spree.

Ida had originally used a small cereal bowl on the front hall table to store some of these things. She now used a large salad bowl, which was surrounded by months' old magazines, newspapers, wallpaper samples and cassette tapes.

She was late for her dinner date and looked in her purse for one of the three address books she kept there; one for work, one for friends and one for family. As she pulled out her family address book, she yelped in surprise. There, trapped between the pages, were the car keys and the house keys she had originally sought. What a relief. She took the keys out and put them on the table so she could rearrange the contents of her purse. This was about as easy as rearranging the inside of a fully loaded moving van.

Ida hurriedly finished and checked her watch. Perhaps she might possibly be on time for her date. She put on her coat, walked out the front door and pulled it shut behind her. This was not a smart move, she realized almost instantaneously. She had left the keys on the hall table.

Oh well, she thought to herself, it wasn't the first time. She'd get in somehow. She could always engage the services of one of the local locksmiths. After all, they cruised past her house every hour or so. She used them so often they gave her frequent flyer points. Getting into her house without a key was like pulling teeth. For Ida, that meant easy.

Don't be a packrat, holding onto that stuff,
Do away with it all, you've sure got enough.

GET RID OF CLUTTER

For over a half century now I've watched office obesity develop into a full-blown, crippling disease. As our office clutter mounts, we're ever more intimidated and frustrated by it. We engineer drainage and removal of water and liquid wastes from society to prevent hazardous buildup, but the effluent that pours into our offices—paper—is never flushed out. DON ASLETT

Clutter piles up. Magazines, letters, brochures, calendars, client files, and invitations pile on, and on and up. You get buried under it all. Perhaps sometime soon you'll clean it up. But for now, "I'll just take this and put it, let's see, here I guess."

Recycle

The garbage basket may not necessarily be the final destination for junk, but anywhere outside your domain should be. Place some items into your recycling bin for pickup. Ask a local charity to retrieve items. Or simply put stuff on your front lawn with a Free Stuff sign and watch it disappear within hours. Don't bother with garage sales. Unless you have a huge accumulation, they can be more trouble than they're worth. Consider the cost of keeping that stuff at your place for weeks, months or even years. The space could be better used, the aggravation could be reduced. Your freedom from clutter is worth a lot more than the few dollars you might make from a garage sale.

Don't Create More Storage Space

The fastest way to fix the problem is to create more storage space. Buy another filing cabinet. Build another bookshelf. Erect another wall unit. Install another desk accessory. Add another tray. But when you do that, a funny thing happens. Perhaps you've noticed that stuff expands to fill the space available for it. Empty space is like a void. Things rush into it.

So what do you do? Stop buying more space, for a start. Set aside a specific time to clean up the space you've got. But don't try to tackle everything at once. The job may be overwhelming, and you'll finish with no satisfaction at all. Choose one area at a time; one drawer, one shelf, and one nook. Commit to cleaning the area. How? Look at all the junk in that space and simply ask yourself some of the questions listed below. If the item fails one of the criteria, get rid of it.

Your "Stuff" Should Meet These Criteria

Examine each item in your workspace and ask yourself:
- Does this item contribute to the positive image that I want to convey? Throw out scandalous photographs, tacky souvenirs and dead plants.
- Is this something I need to operate my business today? Throw out old bulletins, or file them in binders.
- Am I finished with this magazine? Quickly scan the table of contents to see if there's anything you missed. Magazines rarely contain information that will be of long-term reference value. If something is valuable, cut it out and file it.
- Is this part of my current business mission? Throw out or remove items from previous business enterprises that are no longer relevant.

- Do I use this regularly? Throw out office supplies you haven't used in over a year. You can always get more. Avoid saying, "You never know, I might need this someday."
- Does someone else have this information or is it already filed somewhere? Is this spare copy really needed?
- Does this piece of equipment work properly? Throw out old pens that don't work, and fix or throw out broken equipment.
- Is this the most recent copy? Throw out old business cards, pamphlets, letterhead.
- Should this item be filed? Put files into folders for clients or folders for administration.

When in doubt, put items you think you'll want to throw out someday in a bag or envelope. Mark the outside with an expiry date. The date can be long into the future, perhaps two years from now. When the expiry date occurs and you haven't yet used the item, throw it out. The decision will be easy.

TIME TRIVIA

The average adult spends 2.8 hours reading magazines, newspapers and books per week.

STATISTICS CANADA, GENERAL SOCIAL SURVEY

Diary of a File Folder

I'm a file folder. Life sucks. I don't remember much about my early days. Probably wouldn't want to anyway. Suffocating inside a cellophane-wrapped ten-pack, and sitting on the shelf at some big-box business supplies outlet isn't exactly my idea of a good time.

After leaving the outlet I started my first job, storing an agenda for some MBA hotshot. He was working on a new real estate deal. Easy stuff. Just a few sheets. Lots of travel. I got picked up and taken to meetings all over the continent. It was fun, but I'll tell you, some of those guys who handled me smoked their stinky cigars at posh restaurants. Yuck! Made me want to puke. Then the travel eased up a bit. I found myself spending more time in boardrooms right here in power-broker city. Plush seats and mahogany walls—my kind of living. Work got a little more interesting. I started carrying more stuff. A couple of proposal drafts, some meeting minutes, the usual kind of thing. One time I got to carry some big checks—now that made me feel pretty important. And so I should. I'm not just a folder, I'm a document management system!

Then one day, some dork pulled a really dopey move. He misplaced me. I had heard about this from one of my buddies.

It's a pretty humiliating experience. It was really bizarre. I got stuffed inside another file folder. My owner couldn't find me for days. The only good thing was that I carried on an affair with a fine red, card-stock folder—B2 special. She was a beauty. Then some no-brain found me and we were separated. Bummer.

That's when the trouble really started. The proposals became thicker and thicker. Nothing too overwhelming, I thought at first. But I began to put on weight like you wouldn't believe. Fat? I'm talking tubsy. Fatso. Bloato. Bursting at the seams. I was never designed for this kind of strain. The stress really got to me. I lost all the stiffness in my fold and started getting a little ratty at the edges. What did they think I was? A cabinet? I was carrying around research information, supplier lists, city bylaws, plans, you name it. They were really pushing it. But I've got principles. I'm a one-subject file folder. I like to keep things clean and uncomplicated.

Luckily, things started quieting down for a while. Then disaster struck. It was every file folder's worst nightmare; I got misfiled in a cabinet. Wrong alphabetical letter. What dunderhead could mistake the letter b for p? Some idiot assistant put me in the wrong filing cabinet, then left the company. What a jerk brain. People were going nuts trying to find me. I did my best to grab their attention, but somebody had used a pencil to label me. And being so fat, I couldn't even stick my label out far enough for anyone to see.

Eventually, someone found me and it was back to work again. Some smart alec finally got it into his little pea brain to bring on one of my cousins. So we split the work. I was down to the final proposal by now and was still pretty thick but not as busy. I had finally lost some weight.

A few weeks later, I went into semi-retirement. The project stopped or got canceled, or who knows what. It doesn't matter to me. I was taken down to some huge cabinet down in the basement where it's dark and kind of damp, and there's no action. Well, at least no one bothers us much. But working conditions are the pits. Some of my old pals get to laze around in hanging files in the next department, while I and my friends have to sit directly on a cold metal cabinet. My spine's killing me. And we're packed in like sardines. I wonder what the sardines are saying. Probably "We're packed in like file folders" or something. Jeez. No respect. So we just sit in the dark and reminisce about the good old days. Maybe I'll come out of retirement sometime. Could be nice for a laugh or two.

The other day I heard a horrible rumor about some deadly new technology. Apparently, a couple of rows over, some of my buddies were taken out, and everything in them was photographed, or scanned or something. And then poof. End of the line. Off to the dreaded recycling bin. No severance, no job, no future. It hasn't got to us yet, but I'm worried. I was just getting used to it in here. Oh well, a job's a job. And I guess everyone's gotta go sometime.

Don't leave your papers all stacked in a pile,
Sort through them now and learn how to file.

FILE PROPERLY

> *Our two greatest problems are gravity and paperwork. We can lick gravity, but sometimes the paperwork is overwhelming.*
> DR. WERNHER VON BRAUN

The purpose of filing is to keep information that may be valuable in the future. Hence the first principle of filing: if you aren't going to need it someday, throw it out now.

Establish a File Retention Policy

The challenge is in deciding what you'll need and what you can discard. Legal documents, personnel files, contracts and historical records must be kept. Check your office protocols or procedures to find out which items should be kept. Suppliers' brochures, drafts of proposals, printouts of computerized reports and internal memos need not be kept.

Establish a policy beforehand on what you want to keep and for how long. Specify, also, the routine items that can be thrown out or recycled. This way, decisions are easy to make about most items. Make sure the person who is doing the filing knows these policies.

Create Order

Use hanging folders to hold manila folders. Look for items that seem to have the same theme, and create a file folder for them. But don't create too many mini-files. It is better to have a small number of files.

Don't create miscellaneous files, as they are a lazy way to avoid making a decision about what should be done with the information. Not only that, but the file will become a tempting dumpsite for just about everything. The only exception is a junk file described in an earlier chapter. It can be a catch-all for various papers, usually items that don't relate to a particular project. But this file should be placed close by, and you should sort through it at least once a week.

Keep close at hand all the files that you use often. You should have a desk drawer available where you can store a few inches of active files. Desk drawers are for active projects and reference materials, not long-term storage. So when files pile up that you rarely use, move them into remote filing cabinets.

Write a throw-out date directly on file folders, even if it is years away. When that day comes, the decision to discard will be easy. Avoid the temptation to buy more filing cabinets without first finding existing space and throwing out redundant files.

Monthly tickler files are no longer necessary for scheduling follow-up calls if you're using contact management software. But you may need them for paper files, projects, invoices to be paid, follow ups and so on. Thirty-one file folders can be filled with action items for each day of the month.

At work, separate "personal" files from the rest. Personal files would include training materials, lists of contacts, articles, performance reviews and congratulatory notes. If ever you had to leave the company quickly, these would be easy to take with you. Label them clearly so that they won't be questioned on your departure.

One last point about throwing files away; there are plenty of dumpster divers out there mining for nuggets of gold. If it's a sensitive file, it should be discarded properly, through either a shredder or a commercial service that handles bulk shredding jobs.

Electronic Files

Computer files are just as important to keep organized as paper files. The difference between paper files and computer data is that the cost of keeping an electronic file is incredibly small. Purging old files will save a bit of space on your hard drive, but the time to go through them all may not be worth it. More important than purging is creating a logical system of directories. For instance, documents can be stored by year, product or client. Make these decisions early, and when a directory has too many items, perhaps more than fifty, it's probably time to divide it into sub-directories.

Erase drafts as you go. Put the documents you know you'll want to purge in a temporary file. The most important point about computer files is to back them up regularly. Ideally, you should have off-site storage. Ask yourself, "How much would I mind if this work was lost?" If the answer is a lot, then it's time to back up.

TIME TRIVIA

When asked, "What can be done to enhance your productivity?" the five most popular answers among office workers are:

1. *Increase staff to delegate to, or increase administrative support.*
2. *Increase computerization.*
3. *Improve time management and organizational skills.*
4. *Reduce paperwork and administration.*
5. *Increase training.*

PACE PRODUCTIVITY RESEARCH

The Epic of the Hold Button

Aldous's toaster looked as though it had been given a bad enema. In only thirty seconds it had ingested a frozen Pop-Tart, burnt the pastry to a crisp, thrown up a flurry of crumbs and leaked an ooze of gooey raspberry filling from its underside. All this while creating an incessant buzzing that sounded like a cross between an electrocuted cat and a sickly vacuum cleaner.

Phone in hand, Aldous called the manufacturer's twenty-three-hour emergency hot line. "Good morning, you have reached Tooley's Toasters. All our operators are currently engaged. Please hold." Engaged? Aldous wondered. How could an entire department be preparing for marriage at the same time? Just then a voice came on the line.

"Thank you for holding, may I help you?"

"Yes," Aldous began, "I'd..."

"Could you hold please?" The voice cut him off before he had a chance to explain any further.

"Good morning, Tooley's Toasters, warming up a better morning for you than yesterday. How may I help you?" sang a cheery voice.

"Yes, thank you, as I was saying, I'd like to get my toaster fixed.

You see, it has a small adjusting knob at the back and the knob..."

"Could you hold please?" Click. Aldous's temperature increased.

"Good morning, Tooley's Toasters, warming up a better morning for you than yesterday. How may I help you?" Once was amusing, twice was grating.

"Yes, I was just explaining that my toaster has a problem. You see..."

"I'll connect you with the service department." Click. Aldous waited, a bit more impatiently than before.

"Yo, shipping!" shouted a voice in the way that only a busy shipping clerk could.

"Oh, uh, well, I was trying to reach the repair department. You see, my toaster's broken," explained Aldous.

"Yeah, hold on, I'll connect you. Yo, Snotty, what's Repair at? Some dude's got a busted up toaster." Click. Silence. A minute passed. An eternity passed. Aldous grew a beard.

Finally, just as hell was about to freeze over, "Customer service department. May I help you?"

"Yes, you see my toaster's broken." Aldous spent the next four minutes explaining his dilemma.

"Yes, well that's not my department, and I'm sort of busy filing my nails right now. Perhaps you could call..."

"What? Hold on!" Aldous interrupted. "Aren't you customer service?"

"Yes, but we don't handle repairs. I'll transfer you." Click.

"Repairs. Can I help you?" growled a voice that sounded like it was totally disinterested in helping and would have preferred to be working on a stamp collection.

"It's about my toaster. It's got a problem." Aldous's tone was becoming more assertive.

"No problem. Have you talked to Customer Service yet?

They have to give you a work order number. I'll put you through." Click. Silence. Some clicks have that indisputable sound that one hasn't been put on hold but, instead, has been cut off entirely. Aldous realized he was in that never-never land of not quite knowing. The silence had an eerie kind of foreboding to it. The kind of silence that any second would break into the dull monotony of an unforgiving dial tone. In silent resignation, Aldous waited. And waited. Then the inevitable occurred. Click. The dreary hum of an uncaring dial tone.

Aldous decided to take matters into his own hands. He pulled out the toaster's instruction manual, which was written by a Japanese engineer and translated by a high-school dropout. "Please get turned on," it began. Well, Aldous though, I can always give it a good kick. Oddly enough, that was exactly what page 58IIc recommended: "Press toaster with limb hard." Two fruitless hours later, Aldous's dabbling had worsened the toaster's functions, though it would probably do a passable job as a paperweight. He decided to throw it into the trash compactor. But not until tomorrow. Perhaps then the gods of technology would be more kind.

When looking for service, be firm and polite,
Empathetic and clear, don't look for a fight.

GET FAST SERVICE

The Difficult is that which can be done immediately; the Impossible that which takes a little longer. GEORGE SANTAYANA

The key to getting good service is to be polite yet assertive, without crossing over into aggression. Ultimately, good manners will save you time and create better and longer-term relationships. People will usually help if you are empathetic to their own needs, interests and limitations. Ask for assistance, rather than tell someone what needs to be done. Most people love to help, if they can.

Find Out Who Can Help You

When you call for service and someone first answers the phone, ask for the department you want right away. Don't explain your needs to the first person who answers. Their job is to direct problems, not solve them. Call at a time when others are less likely to call. With twenty-four-hour service available, late at night may be your best bet.

Never allow yourself to be transferred without finding out one extra piece of information. For example, find out the person's name to whom you are being transferred or the number for their direct line.

When you get through to someone, use silence effectively.

Ask a question, and wait for the person to solve the problem. Try occasionally saying, "So, what does that mean?" Say this when you're given a less than satisfactory answer.

Don't Let Their Problems Become Your Problem

Your query may not be what someone at the other end wants to hear. In a survey by Pace Productivity, employees were asked what things outside of their control get in the way of their productivity. Among the highest-ranked items were customer calls, requests or emergencies. So, in many cases, your request is actually considered an interruption of someone else's day.

As a result, people will often tell you what a problem you're causing. "I can't put you on hold because that would tie up our fax line." Or perhaps they may use the infamous, "That's not my department." They don't always use exactly those words, but the net effect is the same.

How do you overcome their reluctance to help? In this case, a simple "So?" on your part can work wonders. Another killer comment you might try is, "That's OK, I don't mind." Illogical as it might seem, there's not much of a retort available to the person at the other end. Instead of the request being a big problem for them, you've turned it into a big problem for you, except that you don't mind.

Insist on a Satisfactory Solution

Another question that usually gets action is, "What would have to happen...?" For example, "What would have to happen to get these parts delivered by Monday?" If the company has previously let you down on one of their commitments, insist on an answer that is to your satisfaction. Keep asking the question in different forms until someone gives you an answer. Say, for example, "OK, I understand that no one is around, but let's just say the parts were to arrive here on Monday. How would your company go about making that happen?" Don't just complain. Know exactly what you want to have done.

When the respondent agrees to do something, beware of "I'll try my best" as an answer. This is simply an excuse to fail. If you're not satisfied, ask in return, "What will happen if your try isn't successful?"

When someone offers to call you back later, ask to wait on hold instead, while they do what they need to do for you. If they must call you back, insist that they agree to a deadline, and tell them what kind of message to leave if you will be unavailable or are on another line. If they don't call you with an update by the time you both agreed on, you have another bargaining chip when you need more direct action later. If someone can't meet a deadline to give you an update, how do you know he or she won't break other promises?

Finally, don't forget that two magic phrases can make all the difference: "Please" and "Thank you." Say please when you make a request. Thank people when they do something well.

TIME TRIVIA

Office workers were asked, "What things outside of your control get in the way of your productivity?" Their top five responses are:

1. *Paperwork and administrative tasks*
2. *Customer requests, problems and complaints*
3. *Traffic and travel*
4. *Meetings that are too numerous, too long or unnecessary*
5. *Computer problems and the system going down*

SOLVING PROBLEMS

Trials of the
Tennis Ball Buyer

"Thirteen hundred and forty-three players," Adrian Pritlove muttered to himself. "How in heaven's name am I going to figure this out?" Adrian wasn't sure what heaven's name was, but if he knew it, he'd be sure to ask for help. Out of habit he inserted the blunt end of his pen between his teeth and began gently nibbling. Scarred with tiny teeth marks, the pen was twisted out of shape from constant gnawing. Adrian had chewed through seventeen pens in the past two weeks.

With pen firmly in mouth, he stared at the front wall of his tiny cubicle. On the walls numerous computer print-outs were crudely thumb tacked into a long serpentine ribbon and covered with scrawls of geometric patterns. The interwoven figures resembled ravenous spiders eager to devour anything in their path, including the cubicle itself. They were actually a playoff schedule for the company's annual tennis tournament.

As part-time social coordinator, Adrian's task was to obtain supplies for the tournament. The job was a welcome relief for Adrian. As a full-time audit officer, he spent his time frustrating legions of co-workers by tracking, cumulating, statistically analyzing and reporting the number of paper clips used per hour and the incidence of words beginning with the letter x in E-mail correspondence. (The outbreak of a case of xenophobia in the order-entry department had caused an entire weekend of overtime for his audit group.)

So Adrian was eager to take on extra assignments, such as proudly removing surplus staples from the company's eighty-nine bulletin boards. The tennis tournament, coming up in two weeks, was another opportunity to brighten his routine job. But arrangements were going awry and Adrian was beginning to feel an impending sense of doom, characterized by bouts of profuse and unpredictable sweating. The pressure was getting to him. Or perhaps someone had turned up the heating system.

Scribbling away on the rather daunting charts, he let out a huge moan. Bernice Crampsey, from the office next door, stuck her head into his cubicle. "I beg your pardon, did you grunt or did the air conditioning just turn on?"

"I just can't seem to figure out the tournament," he said.

"What's the problem?" Bernice asked.

"Well, for each game of the elimination style playoff, a new set of balls is needed. I have to order them, and that means calculating how many games are played through all the rounds. D'Souza made up the draw sheet, but he took it away with him on vacation, and he won't be back until next week. So I have to figure out how many games there will be by myself. I've been at this for hours and it's really bugging me."

"Sounds like you've met your match," Bernice giggled. "Isn't there a simple formula for figuring out the number of games?"

"There may be, but I sold my statistics books for a down payment on an electric bed vibrator, so I don't know the formula. And this chart is just complicating things."

"Did you try talking to Crispin Quirty? This sounds like something he could take care of. He's the Director of Eclectic Anomalies."

Adrian was perplexed. He thought he knew all of the more

curious department names in the organization. There was the Department of Quality Operational Inspection Services and Control Operations. Everyone there was named Jones. In the Advertising Marketing Communication Services group, employees always seemed to be wearing ties stained with stale infant regurgitant. Finally, the Office Maintenance Systems Upkeep Coordination Engineering Group was a group of janitors who kept track of paper towels. But Adrian's forays into the company's organizational layers hadn't yet uncovered the Department of Eclectic Anomalies.

"Eclectic Anomalies?" he asked. "Sounds like a store where they sell extension cords. Were they responsible for rearranging the bulletin boards?" Adrian was still upset after spending so many hours removing staples, only to see the boards replaced with new units.

"You go to Quirty if you need a creative solution." Julia said. "Try him." Adrian arranged a meeting through Quirty's secretary, and asked her for directions to the department.

He scribbled notes furiously as she replied in her amiable British accent, "Right, you just go up to the third floor, left off the elevators, right after the second door, down the corridor to the end, exit to the door on the left, down a short flight of stairs, through the gate, past the water cooler, down the hall on the right, then go straight ahead, and it's just on the west side. You can't miss it."

Adrian missed it. He wandered down endless corridors, past monotonous cubicles, through countless doors that locked behind him, down forgotten stairwells, and right by a feisty sales manager's office six times. The sales manager became more perturbed with each circuit, finally offering to steer Adrian in the right direction. Unfortunately, she only made matters worse, costing Adrian an additional three trips past a woman in the credit department who had been eyeing Adrian for weeks. She was always anxious to discuss her paper clip consumption "at a more convenient time, perhaps this evening?" Adrian avoided her and stopped a clerk from the mail room to ask directions.

"Excuse me," Adrian queried, "can you tell me where this hallway goes?"

"Nowhere," answered the clerk. "It stays right here all the time."

After forty-five minutes of frustrated meandering, Adrian arrived at Quirty's office. The door opened before Adrian had a chance to knock, and a smiling face beamed. "Ah, my good man, I was expecting you."

Adrian marveled at his seemingly telepathic powers. "How did you know I was coming?"

"Well, you've already walked past here four times."

Crispin Quirty was wearing another of his incongruous outfits: a red, checkered bow tie, yellow shirt and pale green blazer. He looked like a walking flag from one of the many Central People's Republics that came up endlessly on the old Mission Impossible television series. Light brown hair was slicked back, but a few wayward strands drooped lazily over his forehead. Quirty looked up as if peering over a pair of reading glasses, though he wore none on his long beak-like nose.

"What can I do for you? We're here to help you help yourself with all the help you need," said Quirty, sounding like a public-service announcement, minus the catchy guitar riff.

"I have a problem that needs solving."

"A problem that needs solving? No, no, no, that couldn't be. Every problem already has a solution. The solver simply hasn't found it yet. Do you remember Michelangelo's sculptures, so painstakingly accurate and so gloriously rendered? When he visited the quarry to choose his stones, he already saw his sculptures in them. The sculptures were like solutions waiting to be found. Michelangelo's vision liberated the forms from the pieces of marble that imprisoned them. Just as we must see solutions waiting to be liberated from their problems. All made easier by the infinite and wondrous power of the mind. But I digress. Do you know the winning lottery numbers from last night?"

Adrian confessed he didn't and described the tournament dilemma.

"That's simple," said Quirty. "You just have to take a new perspective on it. The way you described it, you started at the beginning of the tournament and tried to determine all the winners and how they would progress along the path to eventual victory."

Adrian said, "Sure, what was wrong with that?"

"Yes, but how about looking at it from the other end, from the losers' point of view?" Quirty began pacing in long strides. The office was narrow, so he was forced to make quick turns after every couple of steps to prevent his gangly body from crunching into an unforgiving wall. Step, step, turn; step, step turn; like an overgrown cuckoo darting back and forth in front of a clock.

Quirty continued. "In each game, there can be only one loser, right?"

"Yes," Adrian answered cautiously.

"And in fact each loser requires one set of tennis balls, right?" Quirty began his pacing again, step, step, turn; step, step, step, thunk, as he collided with the wall, having missed a turn.

Adrian felt embarrassed, but didn't say anything. As the pacing began anew, he asked, "All right, so where does that leave me?"

"Well, in your tournament you've got one winner and a bunch of losers, each of whom loses only one game. Put differently, you play until you lose."

"Sounds like my love life," Adrian commented.

"So how many losers are there?" Quirty asked.

"Well let me calculate…oh, wait a minute. One less than the total, I guess. Thirteen hundred and forty-two. And if every loser only needs one set of balls, then we need…I get it, thirteen hundred and forty-two sets! Simple."

Quirty smiled knowingly. "Sometimes the best solutions are the simplest. To quote Edward Murrow, 'the obscure we see eventually, the completely apparent takes longer.' You just had to find a different way to express your problem. To quote John Dewey, 'a problem well stated is half solved.' And to quote myself..."

"Yes...?" Adrian waited for the inspirational thought.

"Well, at the moment, I can't think of anything important I've said, but I'm sure I must have said something of value. Wait, how about this? You can clean your socks all you want, but you'll still have smelly sneakers."

"What's that got to do with problem solving?" Adrian asked.

"Absolutely nothing. I just felt like saying it. Now, good-bye. I have a busy day."

Adrian decided to try a different route back to his desk. Opposite Quirty's office he went through a door and froze in place, staring ahead in total amazement. There, directly in front of him, was a small cubicle, like many others in the building, distinguished by pages of stuck-together computer paper affixed to its walls and by a haphazard collection of gnawed ball-point pens. His own cubicle.

Adrian sat down and called the local sports store. "Tennis balls?" a salesman answered. "Yes, we can get four hundred cans for you in three weeks. But that's all, I'm afraid. We just sold about a thousand, not quite ten minutes ago." What in heaven's name is going on, Adrian wondered. He sighed in frustration, looked toward heaven, gave it a name, and quietly amputated a piece of his pen.

Recognize blocks that make it so tough,
Get rid of the shackles to get out of the rough.

RECOGNIZE BLOCKS
TO CREATIVITY

> *Unless the company is endowed with individuals*
> *who challenge old practices and, when*
> *necessary, violate company rules and policy,*
> *it won't be able to meet the difficult challenge*
> *of changing conditions.* THOMAS V. BONOMA

When trying to solve a problem, you may find yourself struggling over and over, attempting the same fruitless pursuits to no avail. What a time waster. What may be holding you back are blocks to effective thinking. If you can recognize what they are, you can change or reverse them. The way to a solution will then become clear.

Thinking blocks fall into three categories: (1) personal blocks are what you bring to the problem in terms of prior knowledge, attitudes or prejudices; (2) problem-solving blocks are the techniques you use that may be limiting you and (3) organizational blocks are those more widely associated with other people or with the organizational culture.

PERSONAL BLOCKS
Fear of failure
Lack of self-confidence or fear of criticism discourages us from

risk taking. But failure is as necessary as success in learning. No child would ever learn to walk if he or she feared failure. Sometimes, you should push yourself to take a risk, asking yourself beforehand, "What really is the worst possible negative consequence that could occur?" Chances are, it isn't much.

Conformity

The conformists' perception and judgments of individuals or organizations can become faulty. "That's the way we've always done it" is the usual conformist statement. Contrarian thinking, or going against the flow, can put you in a unique position for success. For instance, sometimes it makes sense to sell a hot stock just when everyone else is buying. After all, not everyone can win, and, besides, stock prices can't keep increasing indefinitely.

Emotional Numbness

This characteristic is also known as allergy to ambiguity. People like order, structure and routine, and they dislike ambiguity. They don't like to imagine or fantasize, and they are told to "keep control" or "be rational." This kind of thinking results in pedestrian or lowest common denominator thinking.

Stereotyping

Stereotyping is bringing previous ideas, perceptions and attitudes to new situations. It is associating an individual characteristic with the whole. Just because one person is a certain way doesn't mean everyone in his or her group is the same way. This block is also manifested as "functional fixedness," where objects are seen as serving limited functions. A brick for example, is seen as only a building block, even though it can perform many other functions.

Perceptual Flaw

This trait is the inability to see the forest for the trees. It's a difficulty in seeing patterns. There are lots of facts out there, but how do you see the trends that emerge from them?

Attitude

A negative or defeatist attitude can result in an unwillingness to try new approaches. Some people are simply stuck in ineffective routines.

PROBLEM-SOLVING BLOCKS

Lack of Understanding

There are many times when you may incorrectly define the problem or see only a narrow aspect of it. You may be limiting yourself by not going outside the usual boundaries and constraints. On the other hand, perhaps you're tackling too large a problem.

Failure to Think Through Solutions

It's easy to grab the first idea that comes along or to jump to conclusions. This often results from not gathering enough information or from incorrectly identifying cause and effect.

Inability to Suspend Judgment

Generate the ideas first, and evaluate them later. Some people try to evaluate ideas as they generate them. This process inhibits creative thinking and novel solutions.

Ownership

Once someone thinks up a new idea, he will stick with it, even when the evidence indicates it is a bad idea.

Habit Transfer

When you use old approaches to familiar problems, you'll probably be successful. But the same approaches applied to new problems might prove limiting.

Intolerance of Complexity

You might be prone to rely on simple solutions. For instance, some people would like to reduce violent crimes by using longer jail sentences as a deterrent. Life isn't always that simple.

Incessant Effort

Spending too much time on a problem may be detrimental. It may need an incubation period. Take a break, then work on the problem later.

ORGANIZATIONAL BLOCKS

Channels, Approvals and Policies

Red tape gets in everyone's way, and it should be cut. Many protocols and procedures may have outlived their usefulness. You need to understand why they were first introduced, and if there is no longer a reason for them, they should be dropped. For instance, in a well-known, high-tech organization, staff engineers were responsible for qualifying suppliers. They billed their internal clients by the hour for their time, yet no money ever exchanged hands. Also, the client groups virtually ignored the hours they were billed in deciding what resources they were going to use. As it turns out, the billing system cost the equivalent of two full-time people in a department of sixty-five. It could be eliminated.

Resource Myopia

You may not be using all the available resources that are at your disposal. Try getting input from other departments and colleagues. Use materials for different purposes. For instance, a coat hanger works well to open locked automobile doors, in a pinch.

Clinging to the Established

"Why change when things are going well?" and "If it isn't broke, don't fix it" are comments that can result in complacency.

Killer Phrases

You hear these all the time—the negative reactions that say stop instead of go. "We tried that before." "This won't work." "My boss won't approve." "It's not proven." "It's not in the budget." Challenge each one.

Competition versus Cooperation

Avoid win-lose thinking and encourage win-win thinking instead. Departments aren't in competition with one another. They're all out to serve the customer together.

TIME TRIVIA

The average person spends one hour and eighteen minutes per day eating.

STATISTICS CANADA, GENERAL SOCIAL SURVEY

When a distinguished but elderly scientist states that something is possible, he is almost certainly right. When he states that something is impossible, he is very probably wrong.

ARTHUR C. CLARKE

Confessions of a Chain-Letter Breaker

U ntil now, I had never received a charitable request from a client. This request had come by way of a large envelope, filled with a thick wad of photocopies and an official-sounding cover letter. Apparently, a young boy suffering from terminal cancer was trying to set a world record by collecting business cards. I was being asked to help by sending him mine. Something struck a chord in my memory bank about another child's quest a few years back. But surely my client wouldn't be sending an outdated request. This was a new kid, a contemporary copycat card collector.

As an olfactory enhancement consultant (a stinkman to my friends), most of the correspondence between my clients and me goes one way. I send them proposals, newsletters, articles of interest, invoices and smelly stuff. If I'm lucky, they send back checks, but not much else. So my reaction to this unusual solicitation was part flattery, part obligation. I was one of a chosen few deemed important enough to help. Perhaps my client detected in me some altruistic streak.

However, the request wasn't exactly simple. After sending the young boy my business card, I was to send the letter, in turn, to ten of my own associates, along with a list of their names. And I was to include photocopies of all the previous recipient lists that had been sent to me. This was a combination chain letter and corporate charity drive. I had been especially chosen to help.

Among the photocopies sent to me, I counted eighteen pages of previous recipients! They included a veritable corporate who's who, a pencil supply company, a mayor, half of the travel industry and a sludge removal specialist. My kind of guy. Flipping through the lists, I noticed that the photocopies became fainter the farther back I went. After all, the oldest was the eighteenth copy of a copy. Each list had a proud pronouncement at the top, "So and so company has sent letters to the following…" as if the corporation had officially sanctioned the program.

I wondered why I had to copy all the lists I had received. No explanation was provided. Was I permitted to use them for prospecting new clients? Or was I to check them to avoid sending a letter to a company on the list? A quick scan revealed that this rule had already been violated.

Then I began to contemplate what was being asked of me. Sending a business card to a kid in a remote city was easy. But the other part required word processing, a trip to the copy shop, plus stapling, folding and stuffing. Then I'd have to stick and lick. Envelopes, that is. I'd spend perhaps thirty dollars, plus a couple of hours, and some kid would get only a business card. This didn't seem right.

Then there was the staggering effect of compounding. As with any chain letter, if everyone who received a request had complied, the whole planet would be knee deep with these things in no time. Forests were being decimated for a chain letter. But never mind the math, I had been asked to help.

The legitimacy of the request was enhanced by the official-sounding cover letter. You don't mess around when someone links terminal cancer with a book of world records and a children's wish organization. And how could I refuse such ominous phrasing as "I'm sure you are aware that time is of the essence." Then the killer closer: "On behalf of Craig, I would like to thank you for your kindness and support." It was as if my client knew the boy personally. This was important stuff, and I had been asked to help.

As a compromise, I considered mailing my business card to the boy and forgetting the rest of the obligation. But what would happen if my client ever checked up on me? "Say, Harry, did you get that letter I sent you?" How could I turn down him down?

Before taking action, I got to wondering. The request had been through eighteen iterations on its way to me. I figured that if each stage took a week, then the whole thing had started at least a few months ago. Mysteriously, none of the lists were dated, so I couldn't tell when this scheme had begun. Was the kid still alive? Was he getting sick of receiving business cards with out-of-focus pictures of real estate agents? Maybe I could find out.

My only lead was the children's wish organization where the business cards were supposed to be sent. I obtained their number from directory assistance and called. When a woman answered, I began, "Hello, I received a letter about a boy named Craig Sherwood, and..." She interrupted me. "Yes, we have an 800 number where you can get information about that. I'll connect you directly." A recorded message told the story. As it turns out, there had been a young boy with a brain tumor who had been seeking greeting cards, not business cards, though that was in 1989! By 1991, after receiving fifteen million get-well cards, he had been through an operation and evidently is healthy today. The request for business cards that was making the rounds was totally bogus.

So the whole thing was a kind of urban myth turned into corporate scam, perpetrated by no one in particular, just well-meaning individuals with a sense of duty. Its only victims were the good-natured corporations who would overlook all those incidental expenses and wasted time.

Not my company. I would break the chain. I had done it before, and a guy in Venezuela had died. But what should I tell my client? I considered initiating a chain letter in reverse, informing everyone back up the trail that they had been somewhat, shall we say, gullible. Another waste of paper and time. The damage was done. Instead, I called the children's foundation again and made a small donation. I could sympathize with how much this annoyance had probably distracted them from their genuine good work.

As for my client? I hope we keep doing business. Maybe no one will say anything about this. But at least I had been asked.

Don't just believe everything that you hear,
Conduct your research and the answers appear.

ENGAGE IN CRITICAL THINKING

A conclusion is where you got tired of thinking. FISCHER'S LAW

Faulty thinking can lead result in bad decisions. And bad decisions result in wasted time. So save time down the road by engaging in critical thinking now.

Critical thinking is a skill that combines knowledge, skepticism, creativity and analytical techniques. Computers can multiply numbers or sort columns of information or even check spelling. But critical thinking is a uniquely human trait (at least for now) that goes beyond simple logic.

For example, if you look out a window and see water falling, logic and prior experience imply that it must be raining. Critical thinking, on the other hand, adds more observations and conjectures. It allow you to conclude that maybe it's not raining. Maybe it's just someone aiming a sprinkler into the air.

Put the Information in Context
Critical thinking starts with framing the information under examination. What are you comparing the information to? Past experience? Results from other locations? Ideal circumstances? Look for more than one comparison. Check source data and gather as much original information as possible.

Urban myths are an example of a lack of critical thinking that can result in erroneous conclusions. Urban myths never reveal themselves as such. They're stories about facts that could be true, but that aren't verifiable. When the story is repeated, the facts begin to take on a life of their own. How do you recognize an urban myth? Listen for the cue phrase: "A friend of mine heard about somebody…" Chances are the speaker will have difficulty tracking down the source. Rely on verifiable sources of facts, not on hearsay.

Break Out of the Box

Don't rely on information that is convenient and immediate. For instance, many people argue by using a single example, rather than by using principles or general statistics. Look for larger sample sizes and dig deeper for original, first-hand information.

Beware of thinking the same way you did last time. ("We tried that once—it didn't work.") Flexibility is as important as consistency.

Another mistake is to connect events that appear to be linked but that, in fact, are not causal. For example, if car accidents are higher on sunny days, this doesn't mean that sunshine causes accidents. It may simply be that there are more cars driving when the sun is shining, and hence there is more chance for an accident to occur. Watch out for causal links that may not be real.

Be Skeptical of the Experts

Another way the wool gets pulled over our eyes is through over reliance on so-called "experts." In some cases, their expertise may not be as extensive as it seems. For instance, there are some seminar leaders who are excellent communicators and teachers. But they don't always have a solid background in their subject matter. They pick up what they can from their own experience and from popular business or psychology texts, but they don't always have academic credentials.

Other "experts" are often biased. They present one-sided information because it is not in their interest to show the complete picture. Controversial debates about abortion, tobacco or capital punishment feature these kinds of experts. Once you know their bias, you can accept their information appropriately.

Ask Questions

Finally, ask dumb questions. You can't be expected to know the answers to everything. If you're confused, chances are someone else is confused as well. For instance, if you're at a software seminar and can't figure out how a basic operation works, just ask. Others are probably in the same position and will appreciate your question.

TIME TRIVIA

Travel to and from work takes about 5.6 hours per week for the average employee.

STATISTICS CANADA, GENERAL SOCIAL SURVEY

The Myth of the Broken Sprocket

Alastair Beadle was finishing the graveyard shift on the production line for the Boombastic Speaker Parts Division. Alastair was a forty-nine-year-old line operator, though his title was something of a misnomer, as the line was virtually automatic. Just one person was required to monitor the equipment, perform occasional routine repairs and announce weekly raffle winners. Most of the line operators passed the time entering laundry detergent sweepstakes.

Alastair was in the master control chair reading a self-help manual entitled "Fifty-Six Ways to Better Oven Cleaning." Just then, he heard a suspicious click, sprot, thunka sound. It was his stomach, complaining about the large pepperoni pizza he had just finished. Then he heard another click, sprot, thunka, brunkadoo sound. This was not his stomach. It was the production line.

The noise was barely noticeable but incessantly worrisome, as barely noticeable sounds are wont to be. It appeared to emanate from conveyor belt number two on the transport mechanism. It sounded like a kitchen blender chewing up old golf balls. Alastair would know. His kids regularly mangled golf balls for absolutely no reason.

This part of the production line brought together assembled

stereo speakers with the printed cartons in which they were inserted. The cartons were delivered flat, and were popped open by means of an automatic carton machine. A mechanism then pushed the carton over the speaker. Together they moved down the line where glue was applied, and flaps were sealed by pressure rollers. The machine was an engineer's dream.

When Alastair wandered over to the production line, he discovered that one of the small guide bars had bent out of shape, having suffered from metal fatigue. Evidently, it had spent too many late nights watching Aerosmith videos. Alastair had recently transferred from another plant, so he was unfamiliar with the repair procedures. First he tried the time-honored technique that technicians used for mechanical repair. He gave the machine a good kick.

The irritating sound continued. Alastair tinkered with the drive mechanism for a few minutes until he discovered a small plaque attached to the underside of a roller. It read, "If you've been tinkering around and you've just discovered this, you're way off track. Please consult the repair manual." Alastair figured this was probably good advice.

But finding the manual was a major challenge. After searching through numerous filing cabinets, Alastair found the manual in the bottom drawer of the supervisor's desk. He found three volumes actually, totaling five thousand two hundred and sixty-three pages. The index alone was ninety-five pages. There was even an index to the index.

Instead of consulting the manual, Alastair called the emergency help line. He listened as the line rang twice, followed by an auspicious click and a recording. "This is the Dirwinger company automatic repair reporting system. Please remain calm and follow the instructions. Failure to do so may result in loss of one gold star on your monthly report. At the beep, describe your situation, then hang up. Be sure to fill out form nine-three-three-six-two-five-F in triplicate and send copies to your supervisor and the repair center listed on the form. Please wait two to three weeks for a response."

The line beeped and Alastair hesitatingly said, "Hello, this is Alastair Beadle here from line eight. I think we've got a..." His voiced trailed off into silence. He wasn't sure how to describe the problem, but he continued anyway. "Listen, I'm not sure what we've got, but did you know your voice sounds a bit like Jay Leno's? No kidding. Hey maybe you are Jay Leno. Hi, Jay. Listen, I don't think I can wait three weeks. I mean, just listen to this..."

Alastair held the phone out, as if the recording would actually want to hear. "Click, sprot, thunka, brunkadoo," the production line wheezed in the background, slightly louder now. It was showing off for the answering machine.

After a few seconds, Alastair said, "Look, I think I'll fix it myself. Bye." He hung up and returned to examine the guide bar again. A good tug, a few drops of oil, and a well-placed piece of chewing gum on the conveyor belt rollers and all was put right. The unorthodox repair had a marked effect on the production line, as well as on small family of mice that lived in a corner of the plant. The machinery appeared to be working problem free, and fate ticked on.

A problem well stated can often be beat,
But jump to conclusions and you'll end in defeat.

SOLVE PROBLEMS METHODICALLY

Problems can be elusive. The symptoms of the problem are achingly obvious, but the cause may not be well understood. Numerous options for solutions may present themselves. The best approach to getting out of a tangle, particularly in team situations, is to work through a problem-solving methodology.

Review the following steps with the team. Then proceed through the steps, one at a time. Skipping steps is what usually creates confusion later. The first step is to gather some information on the situation. What are the symptoms? What do you know about what is going on? What is wrong? Where does it hurt? Everyone involved should agree on the facts before you formally define the problem.

Define the Problem

The inability to correctly define the problem at the beginning hinders effective problem solving. Management students spend hours in endless debate discussing problem definition in their case studies. But problem definition is not just an academic exercise. It's a real issue that managers, entrepreneurs and technicians need to deal with.

Commenting on problem definition, Albert Einstein said, "The mere formulation of a problem is far more often essential than its solution, which may be merely a matter of mathematical or experimental skill." Well-known thinker Edward de Bono reiterated the point, "Sometimes the situation is only a problem because it is looked at in a certain way. Looked at in another way, the right course of action may be so obvious, that the problem no longer exists."

Ask "How Might We...?"

When confronted with a particularly puzzling dilemma, ask a series of questions beginning with the phrase, "How might we...?" (For example, "How might we build a better mousetrap?")

Challenge the problem statement by asking, "Why...?" (For example, "Why do we want to build a better mousetrap?" Your response could be, "To get rid of more mice.")

Create a new problem statement and repeat the process. (For example, "How might we get rid of mice?" Answer: "To improve sanitation." Question: "How might we improve sanitation?") This exercise could lead to a solution that is quite different.

The problem definition should encompass major opportunities but should be practical. In the example above, for instance, redefining the problem as, "How might we improve working, conditions?" might be too broad.

Select a problem level based on the time available to deal with the problem, the available resources and the degree of commitment.

List and Evaluate Alternative Solutions

Brainstorm a list of alternatives. Use the techniques described in the chapter on brainstorming. Remember to suspend judgment until you have developed a long list of options.

Only when you've developed a list of alternatives should you begin to evaluate solutions. One evaluation technique relies on gut feeling. Ask everyone on your team for a simple yes or no for each item. Add up the votes and see what emerges for each potential solution.

A more formal evaluation technique requires that you first establish a set of criteria. For instance, list such factors as:

- Completeness of the solution. Is it permanent or just a stop-gap measure?
- Approval from others. How long will approval take?
- Availability of other options. Can you wait a few days?
- Short-term cost. What is the cost this month?
- Long-term cost. What is the cost over the next five years?
- Ease of implementation. Can the solution be put in place quickly?
- Customer acceptance. Will customers notice the difference?
- Expertise to handle the change. Are staff resources available?
- Effect on image. Will the solution affect the organization's reputation?

Then rate each potential solution from one to ten on each criterion. Some facilitators use electronic keypads to assist in collecting these evaluations. Participants punch in their scores, which are then directly tabulated by a computer. In this way, the arithmetic of adding up scores from all of the participants is speeded up. There's also more anonymity with keypad scoring systems. With them, participants don't feel embarrassed or ostracized for giving a popular idea a low rating.

The only drawback of this kind of mathematical evaluation is that you may end up with no risk. The wilder ideas tend to be weeded out. Sometimes what's needed is a champion to take one of the more creative ideas and run with it, despite its apparent nonconformity.

The Solution

The range of solutions will narrow down with the evaluation procedure. Then it's time to choose one and implement it. Some buy-in may be necessary, so keep the communication channels open. Let everyone know what you and your team plan to do.

Start with the end in mind, and work back to see what needs to be done to achieve the desired solution. Create a team consensus, then assign follow up roles. Everyone should have a clear task. Once you've put the solution in place, measure the results and, if necessary, start the problem-solving process over again.

Observe Problem Solving Do's and Don'ts

When conducting group problem solving, team members shouldn't have to rely on conjecture or gut feeling alone. There is always an answer somewhere, so the chairperson should encourage participants to make their points using the following:

- Principles. What does the organization stand for? There should be a mission statement to refer to. It can provide a surprising amount of guidance.
- Precedents. What have you done before that worked or didn't work?
- Facts. What information is readily available? You'd be surprised how many different perspectives there might be on the same situation. Aim for agreement on the basic facts before proceeding.
- Comparisons. What are others doing successfully? Look for ideas from other departments or other organizations. If it works there, chances are it will work here.

Counterproductive Techniques to Ignore

Now and then counterproductive dynamics can creep into your team's problem-solving discussions. When they do, try to point them out, and steer members back to principles, precedents, facts and comparisons. Watch out for:

- Group thinking. This is when the entire group gets on the wrong track and is unable to step back and objectively see what the real problem is. Also, minority points of view are discouraged.
- Gut feeling. Some people will express opinions unsubstantiated by facts. There are always facts available, if you look for them.
- Jumping to conclusions and having knee-jerk reactions. Things don't always need to be fixed as quickly as it might seem. Take your time.
- Highly emotional responses. Take time to create calm. Nothing gets accomplished when there is panic or anger.
- Old paradigms. Watch out for people who discourage previously unsuccessful approaches and who avoid new realities.
- Voting for solutions. Building consensus is better than enforcing lopsided votes.

TIME TRIVIA

The average sales person only spends about 25% of their time selling. This represents just under 12 hours per week. The rest of the time is processing orders, providing service, doing administrative tasks, traveling, eating lunch and taking breaks.
PACE PRODUCTIVITY RESEARCH

Junk Food for Thought

Gerald McGuckin was not very knowledgeable about food. For most people, dining is a pleasurable, sensual experience; for Gerald, food was just fuel. In fact, Gerald's idea of exquisite dining was where the self-serve trays came in a choice of colors.

One night, he asked his friend Crispin Quirty over for dinner. Crispin arrived after having stood outside Gerald's door for eight minutes, staring at his watch. His knock on the door was precisely at the allotted hour.

"Hi, Crispin," Gerald greeted him. "Well, I'm told you're a bit of a gourmet chef, so I thought you might want to help me by whipping up one of your great culinary creations."

Crispin walked to the refrigerator and peered inside. The look on his face was somewhere between slight embarrassment and sheer revulsion. "This chicken doesn't look very good," he said.

"Well, no wonder, it's dead." Gerald answered nonchalantly.

"Not anymore," frowned Crispin. "Perhaps we should consider going out instead of eating dinner here. I mean, besides the salmonella chicken, all you've got is half a cucumber, a jug of cloudy apple juice, some stale French toast and a carton of vintage milk."

"The milk should be OK. It doesn't expire until November," said Gerald.

"That was November last year," said Crispin.

"Well, maybe we could make a quiche with the other stuff. I think my sister tried it once."

"You'd probably get arrested for attempted manslaughter. I think not. Let's go out. And could we try somewhere where our order doesn't have to be announced into a microphone?" pleaded Crispin.

They decided on the city's latest trendy restaurant, called The Latest Trendy Restaurant which was just down the street from The City's Trendiest Cafe and next to Just Another Trendy Place. When they arrived, they were astonished to see a group of twenty people crammed into the small vestibule. They waited with the other patrons, exchanging the occasional pleasantry and whiff of bad breath. Twenty-five minutes later they were shown to a table. The maitre'd handed them a menu, and Gerald soon discovered the specials were from the previous day. He caught the attention of a busy waiter and pointed at the menu, "Excuse me, this is yesterday."

"And tomorrow will soon be today," the waiter hurriedly left for the kitchen. "Be back in two shakes of a lamb's tail."

"Lamb's tail. Is that on the menu?" Gerald asked Crispin.

"Yes, along with the dog's breakfast and the cat's pajamas," Crispin answered.

The waiter returned, plunked down a basket of buns and left again. Crispin picked one up, pulled out a magnifying glass, examined it closely, then bounced it off the table. "This is hard as rock."

"Actually if you ask me, hard rock has lost its punch. I'm into easy listening music myself." said Gerald.

Crispin groaned. A few minutes later they obtained a current menu and ordered dinner. The soup arrived first; cream of goat's bladder. As they slurped on their soup, Crispin noticed a nearby table had been sitting empty for a while.

"That's funny," he said, "There are all those people lined up at the door, yet that table is empty. That's money down the drain. I wonder what's wrong?"

"It's certainly not the service," said Gerald as he munched on a succulent eel and horseradish salad. "The bus boys are pretty quick. One of them just removed my bowl before I had a chance to lick it clean."

"Good thing, too," Crispin said. The conversation continued through the main course of broiled goose de la Hudson River covered with a peach melba toast sauce.

As they were eating, a rather overly obsequious waiter dropped by. "How are things? Would you care to have a large bowl of hot soup poured in your lap, while I give you a scolding?"

Both stared at each other in disbelief, then at the waiter. "Well, not really, do you…"

"Oh, I'm so sorry," the waiter looked embarrassed. "I mistook you for someone else. Oh, so sorry. "

"You pour soup on your patrons?"

"Well yes, we have one gentleman whose tastes are a bit unusual, you might say. He's prone to the occasional eccentricity, so we try to entertain him. He likes to bang on his table too. I think he gets it from his former job. You know. Former senator or something."

The waiter left, as Crispin mumbled, "It seems quality isn't a high priority around here. The menus, the empty table, the stale buns, that waiter's mistake. Customers aren't going to be very satisfied."

"But there was a long line up in the front."

"This time yes. But will they come back? I'm not sure if I would."

Gerald and Crispin finished with dessert; a hot and cold concoction called Baked Wisconsin, that was in fact generally lukewarm. A few minutes later, they paid the bill and left. On the way out, Crispin said, "You know, maybe we would have done all right at your place after all. Just one thing. Have you learned how to boil water yet?"

Quality measurements and customer care,
Ignore them today and you take a big dare.

INCREASE QUALITY

Good and quickly seldom meet.
GEORGE HERBERT, ENGLISH CLERGYMAN
AND POET (1593—1633)

The search for quality goes by many names; business process reengineering, total quality management, continuous improvement and no doubt other soon-to-be-invented terms that will enter the lexicon. It's a search undertaken by individuals or by structured teams who strive to satisfy both internal and external customers—put simply, it's giving them what they want in the best possible way. Attention to quality is not just a passing fad. It needs to be an integral part of an organization's value system. By not paying attention to quality, there can be a huge cost in time wasted fixing errors. Higher quality means less wasted time. And, quality can create a competitive advantage.

Define Quality

First, define what quality means to the end users. Find out what the users' requirements are, in terms of what is achievable and what is essential for them to meet their own needs. If you're in the roofing business, your customers may not care what kind of nails you use on the shingles, they just want to stop the rain from pouring into the guest bedroom.

Measure Quality

Measure quality by conducting customer satisfaction surveys, counting the number of discarded parts, tallying unanswered phone calls, tracking how time is being spent and including a toll-free number for problems on your product packaging. Compare your measurements to past performance, industry standards and previous targets.

Set Improvement Goals

Determine goals for quality improvement. Once you've found out where you are today and what your customers want tomorrow, set objectives for improvement, such as a reduction in the number of calls to the help line, less returned product or greater reliability on product performance. Then determine what strategies will get you there and, finally, come up with a plan to achieve your goals.

Become intolerant of defects. Fix them early and fix them at the lowest value-added stage. In other words, check for defective parts when they arrive from suppliers, not when they've been assembled into a product.

Train Others

Determine who is responsible for quality and invest in training. Probably everyone is responsible for quality. "It's not my job" is not an excuse. Empower employees to increase quality. Give them the authority to make decisions, even if that means spending money (within limits) to fix a problem. Employees will make less mistakes if management makes quality a priority. According to Sam Deep and Lyle Sussman, "The units in your organization where the fewest mistakes are made are led by managers who are least tolerant of mistakes... Supervisors need to be taught the art of getting people to give their best. It is their responsibility to empower employees to produce quality."

Build teamwork. Synergy that is created among teams will speed up improvements. Keep communication channels open. Employees need to know where the company is going and how it's doing. One way to increase communications is to reward outstanding improvements. Ask employees what sort of reward they feel is appropriate. Awards might include plaques, employee-of-the-month awards, bonuses or sharing in the profits generated from quality improvement (gain-sharing).

TIME TRIVIA

The average morning radio show host only spends 11 to 14% of their time talking. The rest is music, commercials, news, weather, sports, traffic and station identification.

PACE PRODUCTIVITY RESEARCH

SELLING YOURSELF

It is one of the most beautiful compensations of this life that no man can sincerely try to help another without helping himself.

RALPH WALDO EMERSON

The Lady of the House Is a Man

Having recently lost his job after twenty years, Francois Beausejour wasn't sure what to do next with his career. Management consulting? Equipment sales? Or perhaps something more artistic, like writing jingles for shopping centers? He would need to decide soon.

Just after dinner one snowy evening, he was enjoying a cup of tea before checking what was on television. The choices were uninspiring: one channel showed a program promoting a movie about a highly intelligent yet lovable twelve-year-old child who runs for president. Another channel showed a story about the child actor who had made the movie and who was caught selling drugs in a park. Francois decided to avoid both and settled for a game show. "OK, now for the bonus question," the host announced, "The sun revolves around the earth—true or false?" As an exasperated contestant struggled with the answer, Francois's phone rang. He hit the mute button on the remote control and picked up the phone. "Francois Beausejour speaking," he answered.

"Hello, is this the lady of the house?" the voice on the other end asked.

"No, I'm the man of..." he stopped himself in mid sentence.

"This is Sidney Hackenberger from Starburst First Choice Realty Services International Limited. Would you be in need of any realty services in the next while?"

"No, not really," answered Francois.

"OK, thank you," the voice on the other end of the phone said, hanging up. Well, that was hardly persuasive, Francois thought to himself. The company name was longer than the conversation.

He returned his attention to the television set. A new set of contestants filled the screen. He hit the mute button "…lighter of the two, a pound of feathers or a pound of lead?" the quiz master asked. The camera closed in on a contestant, who was scratching his chin, obviously befuddled. Francois said aloud. "A pound of your dumb head," to no one in particular.

Just then he heard knuckles rapping on his front door. This was odd, since Francois had both a door bell and a door knocker. He opened the door and saw that a few more inches of snow had fallen. A lone figure stood on his porch, with a shovel in one gloveless hand. He had a stubble of a beard and wore a windbreaker that looked too sparse for the harsh weather. His baseball cap proudly announced, "Deposit beer below." The blade of his shovel was narrow and dented, as though he had retrieved it from a garbage compactor. The aluminum shaft was slightly bent. "Oh, hi there," the visitor said. "Well, you look pretty strong so I guess you don't need your path shoveled, do you?"

"No, I'll do it myself," Francois answered.

"OK," the man said, and he turned to leave.

Francois closed the door, nodded his head in dismay. He said aloud, as if reading a news report, "Epidemic strikes. Dumbness spreads."

On the floor, he noticed an envelope he had overlooked from the morning mail. Inside, he discovered a form letter. The first paragraph read, "You'll be the talk of the town in Hudson, as your neighbors on Man Street see you in your new car, Mr. And Mrs. Beaujour." Francois lived on Main Street. And he had been divorced for ten years. He tossed the letter into the garbage.

As it hit the bin it made a clunking sound. The sound struck a chord in Francois's brain. Perhaps it was a G-flat. "Eureka!" he shouted, practicing his rusty Greek. Why were so many people so unskilled at the basics of selling? He decided he could do better. He had twenty years' experience in sales. Why shouldn't he go into the training business?

The next day he began to develop a plan, research the market, establish his goals and outline his strategies for success. Soon he was calling up sales managers, building relationships with them, determining their needs and eventually closing contracts as a training manager. Two years later, his business was growing and profitable. The child movie star, on the other hand, quit the business and disappeared. His name stayed in the public eye only as a trivia question on a quiz show which the contestants inevitably got wrong.

When someone says no make sure you know why,
Help them to make a decision to buy.

MAKE A SALES PRESENTATION

To prevent putting your prospect to sleep, follow the principle of "Don't tell me until you ask me if I want to know." TOM STOYAN

Selling is really about helping a qualified prospect make a decision to buy. At a trade show, a visitor was overheard saying to a pushy rep at a booth, "I'll have to see. You're quite the salesman though." What this really means is, "You haven't connected with me at all and I'm not interested." The prospect appreciated the high-intensity enthusiasm of the sales person, but that energy didn't connect with him.

Follow the Steps of the Sale

When you meet a prospect, proceed through the steps of the sale one at a time. This process starts with a greeting, an amiable introduction that creates empathy and builds the relationship. The warm-up follows, which introduces your prospect to what you're all about, in general terms.

Then comes the qualification phase. Here is where you ask questions, listen and probe to find out exactly where the pain is, what problem you can solve and what benefits you can offer. Open-ended questions get people talking. Questions that can be answered with a yes or a no will bring the process to a halt. On the other hand, phrases such as "Tell me about…," or "Describe for me…" will help prospects open up to you.

Once you've gathered information about the prospect, you can proceed to your presentation. It explains exactly how you plan to meet the prospect's needs. Then you can use a series of trial closes. These are designed to learn under what conditions the prospect would buy. He or she may throw objections at you which need to be answered. Once you have answered the objections, you can try another trial close or a full close again, until you finish with either an agreement to buy or a follow-up meeting or call.

Present Features, Advantages and Benefits

In your presentation, recognize the difference between features, advantages and benefits. What you think is special about your service may be different from what the customer is looking for. Put your sales points in terms that are meaningful to your buyers. For instance, in presenting a health club, you might say, "Our facility has fifteen exercise machines [Feature]. That means there is almost always one available [Advantage]. Therefore, you can get your exercise at your own convenience [Benefit]."

Or, in presenting a new membership dues system for a non-profit organization, "The proposed new dues integrates national and local fees [Feature]. This means less administration [Advantage], and in the long run, there will be more time to increase service to members Your benefits should appeal to people's emotions, pride, prestige, comfort, peace of mind, security, happiness and so on. Remember that most people buy with their emotions but justify their purchase with logic. ('I got a good deal.')"

Handle Objections

Anticipate most objections in your presentation, even answering some of them as you go. ("Now, many of our customers have been concerned about our delivery, but in fact this turns out to be not an issue because…") Have confident answers for all of them. Maintain high enthusiasm.

Develop a "patter," a series of stock phrases and stock answers to questions to keep your presentation smooth. Use personal conviction or anecdotes, plus examples from other customers or clients.

Thank people for their questions or objections. Answer them with a question, if possible. So when someone asks, "When do you deliver?" you can answer with, "What kind of timing do you need?" Or if they say, "How much does your training program cost?" you can answer in return, "How many people are you considering for the program?" Always speak in terms the customer will understand. What's in it for them?

Avoid saying "That's a good question." Find another way to create empathy. For instance, you could say, "I can see how that would be a concern to you."

Use audiovisual aids, but keep them simple. Prospects want to build a relationship with you, not with a slick laptop presentation. When you put aside your visual aids, you can maintain eye contact and watch for subtle body language signaling approval or confusion.

Pepper your speech with questions, but don't make them onerous, such as saying in a presentation to a large group, "How many people here want to make more money?" This question is trite.

At the end of the meeting, create a call to action or next steps. Always know what will happen next after a sales meeting.

TIME TRIVIA

The average length of a sales meeting with a current customer who is already buying product is 37 minutes; with a new prospect, sales meetings average 31 minutes.

PACE PRODUCTIVITY RESEARCH

Journey to the
End of the Block

Sandford Bligenthal pressed the acceleration pedal to the floor, causing his car to bolt along the boulevard. There were only fifteen minutes until his association's meeting started. Sandford figured that the drive would take at least twenty minutes. To say that he needed more time was obvious. To say that he needed more gas was not.

Sandford was urgently looking for a new computer consultant. Twenty-nine years old and an accomplished carpenter, he now operated a swimming-pool maintenance company. He hoped there would be someone at the monthly meeting of his belt-sander drag-racing club who could help him find an accounting programmer. After all, belt-sander drag-racers were into numbers. Revolutions per minute, paper grades, coefficients of track grip. These were subjects of endless debate. Not surprisingly, some of the members still lived in their parents' basements.

Sandford swerved around a truck delivering oversized balloons with "Happy Divorce" written on them. He imagined himself as James Bond, negotiating sharp turns and smashing past the inevitable fruit cart, spilling apples and oranges all over the street to the consternation of an incensed vendor who shook his fist.

Who would catch up to him first? The evil villain or another bad movie cliché? And did anyone have fruit carts anymore?

He checked his speedometer. Sixty in a forty zone was impressive. But then Sandford noticed the Gas Empty light was lit. How long had it been on? He seemed to remember it blinking yesterday. Now the needle was bumping against dead zero. He was running on fumes. This never happened to James Bond.

He drove past a gas station, but it was on the opposite side of the road. A U-turn would be difficult in this traffic. And there was the small matter of the three-foot median in the way. With thirty blocks to go, would Sandford make it in time?

Just then the car lurched twice. Sandford wasn't sure what was happening. He pressed the accelerator to rev up the engine, but nothing happened. Then he realized he was truly out of gas. He rocked his body forward in a series of spasmodic convulsions, as if shifting his weight would coax a few hesitant drips of gas to come out of hiding and sneak into the engine. No such luck.

The engine had no power and Sandford was coasting in a middle lane. But the electrical system still worked. Sandford was consoled that although he was stuck in the wrong end of town, at least he could flip the electric door locks up and down all night.

The car slowed to a crawl. Sandford spotted a gas station, a long two blocks ahead. As he tried to change lanes, a loud, rusty sports car zipped past him on the right, blasting its horn. Right behind Sandford another car flashed its lights. The driver was obviously perturbed, either at Sandford's slow pace or at his Perot for President bumper sticker. Finally Sandford maneuvered across two lanes and stopped in front of a No Stopping sign. Now what? If he could just get someone to help.

He spotted a tall man in his early twenties with a baseball cap and a T-shirt that asked, "Want to Test My Hard Drive?" Sandford caught his attention. "Excuse me, could you give me a bit of a push? I've run out of gas." The man in the cap jumped to his aid and helped push the car to the gas station. "This is great," Sandford said. "I was worried I'd be late for an association meeting. What do you do?"

"Computer consulting," was the response. "Just coming home from a client."

"Do you know anything about accounting programs?"

"Sure do. My specialty."

"That's just the kind of help I need," Sandford said as they reached the gas station. "Give me your card and I'll call you tomorrow."

When Sandford got to the meeting, he discovered that no one knew about computer programming, But at least he had the name of the programmer who had helped with the push. And the meeting was a thriller. Nothing could beat the allure of a number 80 sandpaper demonstration. And Sandford got a great new idea. If belt sanders could race along tracks, maybe Mixmasters could skim across swimming pools. He couldn't wait to find out.

Networking works when you help out a friend,
Consistent behavior pays off in the end.

NETWORK AT MEETINGS

We must all hang together, or most assuredly we shall all hang separately. BENJAMIN FRANKLIN

The most powerful resource in your business may be the relationships you create with colleagues, suppliers, customers and friends. "Know-who" is as important as know-how.

Create a Commercial About You

When you attend a meeting where there is an opportunity for networking, create a fifteen-second summary of what you do and for whom you do it. Use this summary as an introduction. Your statement should arouse people's interest and get them to ask more about you.

Ask people, "If I were to meet your ideal client, who would that be?" This shows you care about their business. Offer to help people by referring them to others. They'll be glad to return the favor.

When joining associations, volunteer to help. People will get to know you better this way. Work on a committee, or offer to present a topic that would be of interest to attendees.

Follow Business Card Etiquette

Business cards are for following up on conversations, not starting them. Be judicious in handing out your card, and do so only if there is a reason. When you receive a card, write a shorthand note on the back it. For instance, "NL" might indicate to send this person a copy of your newsletter. Later, enter the card on your database of contacts, even if that person isn't immediately useful to you. Place each contact in a category, such as hot prospect, client, squash opponent, church group, supplier and so on. Then you can easily look up the category, if someone asks you for a referral.

If someone gives you a business card and you have no interest in following up with that person, subtly fold a corner of the card, or put it in a different pocket. When you return to your office, throw these cards out.

Try to follow up after networking events with a call, a note, a newsletter or an article of interest. Networking doesn't stop with meeting new people. Fostering those relationships over the long term is essential.

TIME TRIVIA

Self-employed consultants spend an average of 2.5 hours per week on networking activities.

PACE PRODUCTIVITY RESEARCH

Waste Nut, Want Nut

Ralph Badger sat impatiently in the television station's green room. He was waiting to tape a segment for a show on the local cable channel. A fifty-five-year-old former salesman for automatic toilet seat lifters, Ralph had recently launched the Remove-A-Nut.

Eight years in the making, it was an ideal device for getting peanuts out of their shells, if you didn't mind lugging around an electrical device the size of a Mixmaster. Now Ralph was preparing for his moment of glory, his fifteen minutes of fame, his hour of power, all in four minute and twenty-three seconds interview. He had managed to arrange an interview on a local cable show after making a series of mildly belligerent phone calls to desperately plead for a spot. After all, Ralph reflected, the media always loved a good invention story. That and anything about alien abductions.

As he sat loading his machine with unshelled peanuts, he was interrupted by the segment producer.

"Hi, you're Ralph?"

"Nuts to you!" he answered emphatically.

"I beg your pardon?"

"Oh, sorry, that's my slogan. I was just practicing it for when

I go on air."

"Yes, well I just want to get the spelling of your name so we can put it on the screen," she said.

"It's Ralph Badger, and the product is Remove-A-Nut, and you can put that it's available at Fred's Fishing Shop, The Sports' Bum Cafe and the Nuts About You Store. The number to call is 1 800 CRACK NUTS, even though the last two letters…"

"I don't really think we can get all that on, probably just your name. Oh, and could you come with me to makeup?" She led him to a nearby room.

Ralph sat down in a swivel chair in front of a brightly lit mirror. The makeup artist greeted him, placed a bib on his chest and began to powder his cheeks.

"By the way," Ralph said to her, "when you do a close up of the product, can you make sure to show the slot where you put the nuts?"

"I do makeups, not close-ups," she responded flatly.

Fifteen minutes later, Ralph joined the host on the set as his segment began.

"So could you tell us how you got started inventing, with a remarkably pithy answer that will warm the cockles of our hearts while sending shivers up our spines?" the host asked.

"Well, I was eating some nuts one night, when I designed the Remove-A-Nut. It's available for fifty-nine ninety-five at fine sports stores everywhere, including Fred's …"

The host cut him off. "My, that's wonderfully fascinating if I do say so myself, which I just did. But it's electrically operated, so how do you take it with you?"

"Oh, I suppose you could have a long extension cord."

"In a baseball stadium?"

"Uh, we haven't worked all the bugs out yet. We're developing a battery-operated version too. We've got a truck battery that'll last about seven minutes. That's enough to crack…"

"Say, that's a smashing tie you've got," interrupted the host as he pointed to Ralph's necktie. "Where did you find it, might I ask, though I don't necessarily need permission to do so?"

"Yes, my dancing peanuts. They're sort of my trademark. Last week, when I was in Fred's Fishing Shop, on Highway 12 where the Remove-A-Nut is available for fifty-nine ninety-five..."

"That's great. Love it. Love you. Love my audience. Love me especially. I'm sure you've got lots of great stories but we have to cut to a commercial. Thanks very much for showing us your, um, nut thing. Will you come back again sometime?"

"Nuts to you! Sure, how about tomorrow?" Ralph answered enthusiastically. "I'll do a demo. You see this little lever here..." His words were lost to an ad for a pet smell remover.

Later that night, the show aired. Ralph anxiously waited by his phone, working on his newest invention, a battery-powered paper clip. Unfortunately, of the thirteen calls he received, absolutely no one wanted to buy a Remove-A-Nut. However, they all wanted one of his neckties with the dancing nuts. Ralph threw his hands up in dismay. If necessity was the mother of invention, maybe Remove-A-Nut was simply an unwanted orphan.

Create an event that will make tonight's news,
Promote your own business while espousing your views.

GENERATE PUBLICITY

A celebrity is a person who works hard all his life to become well-known, and then wears dark glasses to avoid being recognized. FRED ALLEN

The purpose of publicity isn't to attain personal glory or to create sales or leads. Instead, use publicity to increase awareness and credibility. It's similar to advertising, except that you don't pay for it.

Establish the Message and Identify the Audience

When designing a publicity campaign, first decide on your message. It must be newsworthy. Your goal might be to announce a new product, some major research results, business growth or a new factory. What is the compelling hook that will get people to sit up and take notice? No one cares about all the research you put into a new product launch. But they will care if you tell them there is a new way to improve their car's gas mileage.

Once your message is clear, decide what people you want to reach, and target the shows, newspapers and magazines they like. Are you targeting teens or adults? More specifically, do you want to reach high-school students or business owners?

One final point about publicity. You never get paid for it. Some people are naive to think this happens. Not so, unless you're the member of a royal family willing to spill your guts to a trashy tabloid.

Know Where You Want To Be

To get on shows or in print, create relationships with the media. Luck helps. Remember, also, that friends of friends work in the media. Find them. Hire a professional if you have something newsworthy. Professionals know who the contacts are and how to reach them effectively. Meanwhile, keep an eye out for media coverage at conferences or shows.

Create news the media will pick up on. For instance, pull a unique stunt downtown that will attract an audience and the press. If you're launching a new product, find a way to make an event out of it that draws attention to the product and lets people try it at the same time. Be an authority. Send out press releases, write articles, deliver speeches, sit on panels. All of these add to your credibility.

Become a Good Interviewee

Before the interview, hand a cassette to radio station operators and ask them to make you a copy.

Ask when the story will run, but be prepared to be pre-empted. Give the station or paper a phone number where their audience can reach you. Don't tell the whole world about an upcoming appearance, as you might get bumped. Make reprints, but respect copyrights when you photocopy and distribute them. Tape everything. Listen to how you did and improve.

During the interviews, be a good interviewee by following this advice:

- Know what a sound bite is and stick to it.
- Be aware of edit points. Don't drone on.
- Use whole answers to questions. "Follow responses with explanations."
- Practice responding to tough questions with colleagues beforehand and never say, "No comment."
- Never overlap others.

- Be excited, dignified or whatever, but be passionate.
- Try not to disagree with the interviewer. Steer them to the right answer, but avoid saying, "You're wrong about that." The interviewer is the voice of the audience and you don't want to belittle your audience.
- Cover the questions the interviewer might not have asked (i.e., your own agenda).
- Have standard answers to tough questions. You should never be surprised.
- Don't try to turn a TV interview into an infomercial. If the audience members like you, they'll find a way to reach you.

TIME TRIVIA

The average adult American spends 28 minutes a day dressing.

AMERICAN'S USE OF TIME PROJECT,
UNIVERSITY OF MARYLAND

ACHIEVING BALANCE

Do not take life too seriously. You will never
get out of it alive. ELBERT HUBBARD

Always Say No Until Someone Asks

N ow, here was a to-do list to be proud of: Feed Susan's cat, water the Titcombes' plants, deliver an old baby crib to the Smiths, pick up the Natrall's baby from day care and clean out the sludge from a rather intemperate Garburator that had spewed a gallon of gunk on the Walton's kitchen floor.

In the past two days, Samantha Pulleyblank had agreed to all these tasks, leaving little time for her own chores, not to mention her own part-time business. Instead of developing her clientele, she had become the neighborhood handy person. Need something repaired? Call Samantha. She'll fix anything. No job too difficult. Have something slimy that needs exterminating? Samantha will know. Have visiting relatives that you don't really want to see but would love to have taken to the local tourist traps where just maybe some of their precious hoarded pennies might be extracted from them? Samantha knows all the spots.

In between helping her neighbors, Samantha ran an interior design business from her home. She specialized in remodeling bathrooms, equipping them with musical toilet-paper holders that played the opening notes of the national anthem with each tug. She had also developed a unique fold down reading table for use in the bath called the Bath-Tubby-Buddy. It came complete with a built-in telephone, candlestick, cup holder and a belly button cleaning tool. Samantha's other specialty was the miniature bookshelf she had installed next to a number of clients' toilets. Each was stocked with such exciting titles as Decorative Swamplands Revisited, The Collected Works of Howard Cosell, and Principles of Parking Lot Design. Lately, though, she had been preoccupied with a client complaint. Apparently a new automatic exhaust system for removing toilet odors had inadvertently been connected to the client's central air conditioning system. When she got any spare time, Samantha also volunteered as president of the Canoeists and Rafters Against Pollution, also known as CRAP.

The phone rang. It was her cousin Blossom, pleading for help, as usual. "I wonder if you could help. We'll be in town next week and, well, Sydney needs to see a specialist. Ingrown toe nail that's become a bit nasty. We'd like to stay at your house, so you'll need to pick us up at the airport Monday night. Then Tuesday morning you could deliver us to the hospital. And Tuesday evening I have to pick up a painting I've had framed, so I wonder if you wouldn't mind driving me. Oh and perhaps you could buy some stamps for me as well. Maybe two hundred? And if you wouldn't mind paying for them, I'd appreciate it, but I'll need the receipt." Blossom had a novel way of accounting for other people's money.

Later that morning, Samantha arrived at the Titcombes' house to do her daily chores while they were away on vacation. Just feed the plants, she had been told. What she hadn't been told was that the water pipes were acting up. This meant a rather slow dribble of water from the taps, causing each bucket to take about three minutes to fill. This wouldn't have been so bad except that there were dozens of different plants in the house. Thirsty azaleas were zealous for a drink. Undernourished geraniums looked longingly for liquid, and a parched petunia pleaded for provender.

Having taken care of the flora, Samantha followed up with the fauna. She had to feed Harry the dog, along with four cats, three budgies, two hamsters, one goldfish (mysteriously down from two the day before), a small rabbit and a slug, which had shown up uninvited. The instructions, which covered two type-written pages, had annotated footnotes.

The kitchen phone rang. Samantha stared at it, not sure what to do. Well, I'm here, thought Samantha, I suppose I might as well answer it. Could be important. After all, someone wouldn't call without good reason.

"Mrs. Titcombe?"

"No, this is Samantha Pulleyblank, the neighbor. Perhaps I could help."

"You most certainly can. We're conducting a small survey. Could I ask for just a few minutes of your time?" A few would turn out to be fifteen.

"Oh sure," Samantha chirped delightedly. "I'd love to help. The knowledge derived from understanding fundamentals in consumer behavior and the consequences of..."

"Yes, well, no need for all that, Mrs. Titcombe."

"Pulleyblank actually. But I don't live here."

"That's all right, Mrs. Titcombe. Just answer the questions anyway."

The questionnaire turned out to be an excuse to sell house-hold cleaning products. Samantha ended up purchasing sixty dollars worth of spot removers, sink scrubbers and a unique product called Barf-Out, designed to protect carpets from flying projectiles. She wondered what the research company would say when they got around to calling her own house. She'd have to go through the whole thing over again.

After an hour of chores, she returned home, just as her husband, Darwin, was arriving. "What did you do today, honey?" he asked.

"Well, not too much, I guess. I took care of most of the errands for the neighbors. Got a little bit of work done on my proposal. I just wish I had a little more time for me."

"Why do you do all that stuff? What about your own business? Why don't you turn people down once in a while?" said Darwin.

"Oh, no. I couldn't do that. I simply won't say no."

"You just did."

"Thanks."

"By the way," said Darwin, "there's a flyer here for a group you might want to join. It's the Association of National Service Workers Enabling Refinements in Nonchalant Options. I think you'll like their acronym. It's ANSWER NO."

Extravagant favors are a burden, you know,
So don't just give in, be firm and say no.

SAY NO

It's easy to say yes and tough to say no. You feel flattered to be asked. There are so many projects you would like to be able to do, if you only had the time. People often say yes to others because being agreeable is a positive trait. Saying no might hurt someone's feelings. As time management expert Alec Mackenzie says, "Wanting to please is one thing; most of us are people-pleasers at heart. Indeed, the humanitarian instinct to help those in need is a worthy trait. But wanting to please so badly that you lose sight of your own priorities is something else." Especially for people whose self-esteem is low, saying no isn't an option when they feel powerless or undervalued.

But saying yes might lead to regrets later on. You find you're burdened with just too many things to do. You either have to cancel your commitment, delay it, or do a less than satisfactory job. Then, no one is happy.

Be Clear About Your Own Priorities

How do you say no? Simply stick to your plan. If you have a written set of goals and strategies, they'll guide you on your course and give you permission to turn down requests from others. For instance, a financial planner telephones to offer you an investment letter. What do you tell her? If you already have financial goals and strategies, it's easy to say no. "Thanks, but I already have an investment plan, so you don't need to send me a newsletter about stocks."

Some people get themselves in trouble by accepting assignments or favors without understanding exactly what is being asked of them before they respond. When someone says "Can I ask you a favor?" respond with a question of your own. "Can you tell me what you're looking for first?" or "Is it something I can easily fit into my schedule?"

You have a right to say no. Remember that others may take you for granted if you don't. And the more you say yes, the more they'll ask.

Be polite but firm in saying no. You only build false hopes with wishy-washy responses. For instance, saying, "I'll try to be there" in response to a party invitation gives an excuse to avoid a commitment, but it doesn't do anyone any favors.

If you really want to help, provide suggestions or alternatives to the person who is asking. You might say, for instance, "I can't do that task today, but how about next week?" or, "I'm not available, but how about asking John instead?"

When in doubt, it's easier to say no now, then change your mind to a yes later, rather than the other way around.

Deal with Requests from Your Boss

When a superior asks you to do a new and urgent task, remind her that you are working on other projects that she has already identified as top priorities. Then ask for help in deciding where the new task should fall on the list of priorities. You might try asking, "What would you like to give up in order for me to do this?"

When you say no, time management expert Harold Taylor

recommends keeping your answer short, without a lengthy justification. ("I'm sorry, I'm not available that night.") On the other hand, Alec Mackenzie, author of "The Time Trap," says that giving a longer answer with reasons reinforces your credibility. Take your pick.

Saying no keeps you focused on what you do best. It's better to excel at just a few things, rather than to be just average at many.

TIME TRIVIA

Newborn infants sleep 17–18 hours per day. By age 4, sleep drops to 10-12 hours per day and to about 9-10 by age 10. By adolescence people reach their norm, 7½ hours. This drops to 7 hours by middle age and to 6-6½ hours by the seventh decade.

LYDIA DOTTO, ASLEEP IN THE FAST LANE

The Legend of the Busted Van

Friday, June 13

Mr. and Mrs. Will E. Nili,
c/o The Silly Valley Trailer Park and Dog Kennels,
Third row down, at the end near the outhouse,
Highway 7,
Flin Flon, Manitoba
Canada

Dear Mother and Father,

Before your return from vacation, I thought I'd make you aware of a few minor complications that arose while I was moving out of the house. Nothing major, I assure you. Nothing that can't be fixed with a screwdriver and a bit of touch-up paint. And maybe a new wall.

But before I begin, let me again say how grateful I am to have been able to stay with you all these years. As we all agreed, my upcoming forty-third birthday seemed an appropriate time to get my own place.

As you instructed, I loaded my belongings into your mini-van and the old trailer. I should note that at the onset the trailer wasn't in the most pristine condition. In particular, the yoke wouldn't attach to the back of the van. You have always lauded my ingenuity and, once again, this quality was not lacking. Gathering up some old wire, I fashioned a binding mechanism to attach the trailer to the van. Then, with everything packed, I was ready for my grand departure.

I drove the van out of the garage and a short way up the driveway. I'm sure you would give me credit for wanting to get out to check the trailer once again, which I did. Perhaps, in retrospect, it was slightly inappropriate to have left the van in neutral gear, seeing as the driveway is on an incline. As I made my inspection, the whole assemblage of vehicle plus trailer began rolling backwards, picking up speed on a determined journey to the rear of the garage. Fortunately, Dad's workbench was there to bring everything to a standstill. Unfortunately, the workbench is now missing its front section.

I re-entered the van, but unbeknownst to me, the trailer had become tangled in what was left of the workbench. Thus, pressing on the van's accelerator repeatedly resulted in a kind of clumsy lurching, but no real movement. Finally, with a firm press to the floor and a thunderous roar of the engine, the van, trailer and bits of workbench bolted out of the garage, up the incline and across the road.

My quick thinking on the brakes and an expeditious swerve of the steering wheel prevented a head-on collision with Mr. Beausejour's oak tree. His maple tree, on the other hand, was not quite so fortunate. Nor was the van. But the punctured right headlight and a few dented bits of metal are not too great a price to pay for the pristine condition of that venerable oak.

By now the front wheels found themselves in a muddy ditch. Once again, the van was immobile. I didn't want to chance another rapid burst of acceleration, so I opted for a novel solution. To effect a constant velocity, I put the gear in reverse and jammed a briefcase between the seat and the accelerator, causing a steady force to be applied to the pedal.

To add impetus, I exited the van and, with the driver's door open, began to push the vehicle to assist it on its way. My plan was to jump inside once everything was moving. It was an exemplary plan, to be sure. The execution though, was slightly wanting. Sure enough, the van lurched out of the ditch, but faster than I had anticipated. I received a solid thwacking by the driver's side door. Then, with a mind of its own, the van hastened backwards across the street, jackknifing the trailer on its way.

At this point, the laws of physics offered a remarkable display of leverage, torque, and objects in motion. You see, my jury-rigged wire connector snapped, leaving the trailer sitting on the road while the van barreled down our driveway once again. This time, luckily, Dad's workbench was spared. As I found out, though, objects in motion only continue to move until acted on by an outside force. The rec room door, for instance. Well, in fact, a good portion of the wall, as well. But, you had always been thinking about getting it renovated. Now's your chance.

By the way, speaking of doors, the driver's door found itself in a small disagreement with the wall of the house on its way to the garage. And though it tumbled into the flower bed, your precious roses were spared.

I returned to the garage to inspect the minor damage to the rec room. Well, perhaps minor is a slight understatement, all things considered. But, with the new hole in the wall, the rec room is notably opened up.

I examined the dents on the rear of the vehicle. Perhaps in my haste to ascertain the extent of the damage, I neglected the now abandoned trailer. Recall, if you will, that the trailer, full to the brim with my belongings, was in the road, just at the crest of the incline. Once again, the laws of physics were undeniable as the trailer began to roll towards the garage. Actually, roll is a bit mild. Careen might be more befitting.

The hurtling trailer caused only minor damage to the van's front radiator. I might mention that the air conditioning seems to be malfunctioning as well. And maybe you'll want to consider a new engine block.

So how, you might ask, did the windshield end up with a series of web-like cracks? Remember that bowling ball you wanted me to take away? Somehow it became dislodged from its rightful place on the trailer. When the trailer came to a stop, the ball was destined to continue. Physics once again, I presume.

I've omitted one small detail. When the trailer jackknifed at the top of the hill, it also spun around. Consequently, at the end of its journey in the garage, the trailer yoke ended up jammed underneath the front of the van like a wedge, and the van was stuck once again. I reasoned, as I'm sure you would have in the same situation, that if I could lift the front of the van, I could then move the trailer hitch from underneath it. This might return the entire conglomeration to some semblance of order.

I'm sure you would assign full marks for my ingenious plan. I lowered the electric garage door, then attached the van to the garage door by means of a short rope. With calculated forethought, I reasoned that the electric door would raise the van, thereby extricating the trailer yoke. Unfortunately, instead of raising the van, I succeeded in lowering the door, along with accompanying rope, track, motor, wiring, bolts and a small section of ceiling. I must say that this was certainly not a well-built system. Perhaps you'll want to have a few words with the firm that undertook the original installation.

So why, you may ask, am I writing? Apart from the minor damages which I have discussed, to the front of the van, the back of the trailer, the back of the van, the front of the trailer, engine, garage door, flower bed, rec room wall, ceiling, maple tree, van door, workbench and windshield, everything is in superlative condition.

However, there may have been an omen in this slightly inconveniencing series of incidents. After all was said and done, I had the occasion to reflect on the rather unusual events that had transpired. I wondered whether the forces of the universe were attempting to persuade me that my rightful place is not actually outside this wonderfully cozy domicile I call home. Quite possibly, my eagerness to seek a new abode was somewhat premature. As such, I resolved to move my belongings from the trailer back into the house once again. So when you arrive home, I'll be here, greeting you with open arms. I can't wait to see you once again, so that I might relay to you the wonderful adventures of my experience with the dishwasher.

Love, as always, your son Dudley

P.S. You might want to avoid the garage entrance.

P.P.S. Would you mind terribly if I borrowed four hundred dollars?

Stress and anxiety lurk in your mind,
Take more control, and peace you will find.

CLEAR YOUR MIND
OF ANXIETY

---

*The only things that evolve by themselves
in an organization are disorder, friction
and malperformance.* PETER DRUCKER

Anxiety is like stress. It is an internal sensation that people manufacture in their minds. Anxiety is really a response to an external event.

One type of anxiety deals with events that haven't yet happened. You perceive that there might be some negative consequences associated with an upcoming event that is coming up. As a result, you don't do the things you need to do, for fear of these negative consequences. (Ironically, in the previous story, the protagonist exhibits virtually no anxiety. He seems oblivious to the consequences of his actions. But just imagine the anxiety of the letter's recipients!) If you question the assumptions you make about possible consequences, you will have a tool with which you may fight anxiety, and you can get on with what needs to be done. Try following these easy steps in mentally preparing yourself.

Identify Your Assumptions

First, identify the operating assumption that causes you anxiety. For instance, you might think, "People don't like me when I have to ask them for money they owe me." Or perhaps you say to yourself, "Employees don't like to be fired."

Next, determine the consequences you think will occur that are increasing your anxiety level. Perhaps you think:

"If I ask someone for money, she will reject me and I'll feel stupid," or "If I fire the employee, he will become upset and yell at me."

So you think you know what the negative consequences will be. What is your normal behavior? What instructions do you give yourself as a result? Perhaps you tell yourself:

"I won't ask her for the money right now. Maybe she will remember," or "I'll put off firing him, hoping he'll improve on his own."

Change Your Assumptions

The preceding assumptions are simply false hopes. Here's where you need to be a bit creative. Question your operating assumptions and list their opposites. Turn them around from negative consequences to positive ones. In the case of the examples above, you might tell yourself:

"People really would rather pay on time. People like to hear from our company," or "This employee might not really want to be here. Getting fired might be the best thing for him."

Although you can't be sure these positive consequences will occur, you can't assume your original negative assumptions will occur. Things never turn out as badly as your mind thinks they will.

The last step is to determine a success strategy for action.

"I'll present them with their overdue statement in a fun way and make a small joke of it," or "I'll ask the human resource department for some assistance in helping to terminate the employee."

Once you've determined your strategy, make an action plan. Write it down and stick to it.

"This afternoon I will call three overdue accounts," or "This morning I will meet the employee and let him go."

After you've taken action, congratulate yourself for a job well done, reinforce how well the encounter turned out and use affirmations to remind yourself how well you handled the situation.

TIME TRIVIA

The average office worker spends only 3 hours and 42 minutes per week on lunch, breaks and personal business. That's only 44 minutes per day.

PACE PRODUCTIVITY RESEARCH

Ballad of the Subway Stop Blues

The subway doors are closing, then the train begins its run,
It takes its load from here to there, another day's begun.

As Dean looks up he traces out his route upon the map,
His briefcase jammed with take-home work sits neatly on his lap.

The pile of work is beckoning, it doesn't go away
He's got to start to tackle it, not wait another day.

He looks about, his straying glance is fixed upon an ad,
If only he could work his way, those goodies could be had.

The flashy ads for splashy suits and natural food for thought,
He's mesmerized, by chewing gum, twelve flavors to be bought.

He races off to meetings that go on for half a day,
They all start late, the leader's dumb, but what is Dean to say?

The fax machines and copiers and telephones that beg,
To answer them within two rings, for that's the standard reg.

He thinks about his cubicle, he's been there for a while,
His face is stern, his body stiff, he barely cracks a smile.

He contemplates a day of bliss, away from all the deals,
To watch TV and fresh paint dry and try some frozen meals.

There's never time for children's plays or walking with the dog,
The garden's been neglected now, it looks more like a bog.

His tie is stained, his suit is soiled, he has to start at eight,
To get them cleaned would take too long, he'd risk arriving late.

He's been up late, he's reading when his eyes begin to close,
His head drops down, the book falls off, he strikes a restful pose.

He's dreaming of the day when he can take a well-earned break,
To laze around and fatten up and calories forsake.

Back on the train, the subway stalls, it causes much dismay,
A delay could cost the passengers a piece of well-earned pay.

And no one knows of why or how the subway's come to rest,
There's nervousness and fidgeting and hoping for the best.

A tapping foot, an awkward glance, a woman flicks her hair,
An ugly burp, a smelly fart, both putrefy the air.

Dean feels confined, stuck in his seat, he gazes all about,
He's like a rat caught in a maze that's trying to get out.

He looks about, his searching eyes reveal his inner fear,
The guy without deodorant is sitting way too near.

His eyes revert to private thoughts, the normal and mundane,
Of unpaid bills and children's ills, and whether it will rain.

Of cutlery and greasy fries, the sewage in the lake,
Of calluses and smelly socks, how long the train will take.

And in the train the tapping feet and restless glancing eyes,
All search about, transmissions of their silent, worn-out sighs.

But then a sound like grinding gears is heard throughout the train,
The engines start their rhythmic hum, there's movement once again.

Quite slowly first, then building speed, the train rolls down the track,
It shunts away its occupants, a few of whom glance back.

Within the steel and plastic walls, they carry on the day,
From here to there, the passengers continue on their way.

Dean checks his watch, he'll make it soon, the office isn't far,
He tells himself it could be worse—he could have come by car.

**Avoid getting stressed through struggle and strife,
Give yourself time to balance your life.**

CREATE BALANCE IN YOUR LIFE

*Modern man thinks he loses something—time—
when he does not do things quickly, yet he does
not know what to do with the time he gains
except to kill it.* ERIC FROMM

All work and no play leads to disaster. At work, strive to create an atmosphere of hard work balanced by good humor and a positive attitude.

Make time to eat a proper lunch and go for a short walk to clear your mind of tensions. The break distracts you from pressing problems and creates an opportunity for new ideas to incubate. Problems sometimes need to be left alone for a while.

Use humor at the office to maintain positive morale. The jokes that find their way through fax machines and E-mail are a welcome antidote to an overwhelmingly frantic world. Celebrate and encourage them.

Attend social events with those on your team. The information you learn about them at the baseball game or the bar after work will help you understand them better.

Leave Your Work at Work

Well-known time management expert Alec Mackenzie said that "making time for pleasure and fun is not a luxury, it's a responsibility you have to yourself." When you think of your life outside of work, examine how much time you spend in each of the following areas and allocate time for those that are important:

- Physical fitness. Keep your body in top shape to be able to withstand the stress of work. Set aside time for exercise, ideally getting your heart rate up for at least twenty minutes, three to four times per week.
- Family. Your spouse needs your companionship, and your children need guidance and support if they are to lead fulfilled lives. Block time for them if necessary. For instance, you should devote weekends to your family. If you're working both Saturday and Sunday, you should re-examine why you're spending so much time at work. Apply some of principles from earlier chapters to make time for the things that count.
- Community. Your responsibility to the community goes beyond your work. Get involved with a political party or organize a street festival in your neighborhood. Help those institutions that have helped you; raise money for your university alumni, for instance. Work on a project with your service club. The more directly you become involved with others who are less fortunate, the more enriched your own life will become. And remember that your community isn't just the people who have interests similar to yours. Community is about becoming involved with others who have dissimilar interests, but who share a common vision or place. The people you meet from different backgrounds will give you new perspectives you might never otherwise have discovered.
- Spirituality. The time you spend enriching your spirit, whether through meditation, religion or discussion, gives you new perspectives on your career. If you don't attend a

church, synagogue or mosque regularly, take time out now and then to appreciate the richness of life and the forces of the universe that shape and guide you.

- Education. Learning is a lifetime pursuit. You need to constantly improve your skills and knowledge through reading or attending courses. Take a night course, go to a weekend seminar and read a self-help book once per month. Read novels, as well, for they give you other perspectives on humans' place in the world.
- Culture and leisure. Culture enriches, and leisure relaxes. Make time for both. Go to a play, a movie, a concert or a poetry reading. Pack a picnic in the park. Try a different museum every few months. Smell the roses.

Set goals for each area. Then allocate the time you want to spend on important activities and schedule this time in your planner. Block time for important priorities outside of work, just as you do for work activities.

Most of all, keep smiling. Whatever challenges you face, however much the nasty sorcerers of stupidity infringe on your time and on your life, the world will continue on its happy way tomorrow. And you can make a difference—if not for others, then at least for yourself. Remember, your time is worth it.

TIME TRIVIA

The average distribution of time for a seventy-year-old man looks like this:

Sleep	23 Years
Work	19 Years
Leisure	9 Years
Travel	7 Years
Eating	6 Years
Illness	3 Years
Personal care	2 Years
Religion	1 Year

PAUL RICE, TIMESOURCE

Then he waited, marshaling his thoughts and brooding over his still untested powers. For though he was master of the world, he was not quite sure of what to do next. But he would think of something.

ARTHUR C, CLARKE, 2001: A SPACE ODYSSEY

ABOUT THE AUTHOR

Mark Ellwood specializes in helping people make better use of their time. After attaining a Bachelor of Commerce from McGill University in 1978, he spent ten years in product management. He then became an entrepreneur, inventing and launching the TimeCorder® in 1989. This portable, electronic desktop device allows employees to easily track the time they spend on different activities. Today, Mark is a productivity consultant, keynote speaker and trainer. He teaches practical techniques for improving results that can be put to immediate use. He is also founder and president of the Inventors' Alliance, a non-profit group dedicated to helping inventors develop their businesses. He lives with his wife, Susan, in Toronto.

PRODUCTS AND SERVICES FROM PACE PRODUCTIVITY

Seminars and Keynotes

Mark Ellwood's seminars include a high degree of audience participation to create lasting learning. He uses a combination of mini-lectures, group exercises, simulation games and discussions, all spiced with a dose of humor. In his keynotes, he strikes a "chord of familiarity" with audiences, delivering a powerful message that's witty and exciting.

Consulting

TimeCorder® consulting is a user-friendly way to measure and improve productivity. Employees track their time with simple-to-use TimeCorder® devices for two weeks. After they return the units, the information is analyzed and recommendations are provided to the client. Most participants find the process easy and insightful, and they all receive copies of their own results at the end.

More Time for Selling – Audio Tape

Increase sales productivity with this one-hour audio cassette. It includes powerful data on how sales people spend their time, and it provides valuable tips on how to increase sales productivity. An excellent tool for sales professionals at all levels.

Time Tips – Book

This book is a collection of productivity tips, written in point form. It includes topics covered in *A Complete Waste of Time* plus others, such as managing stress, coaching and communication skills.

For any of these products or services, or for additional copies of *A Complete Waste of Time*, contact:

Pace Productivity Inc.
47 Kenneth Avenue
Toronto, Ontario, Canada M6P 1J1
Phone: (416) 762-3453 Fax: (416) 762-3301
E-mail: ellwood@netcom.ca